THE MERCHANT OF VENICE

By WILLIAM SHAKESPEARE

Preface and Annotations by
HENRY N. HUDSON

Introduction by
CHARLES HAROLD HERFORD

The Merchant of Venice
By William Shakespeare
Preface and Annotations by Henry N. Hudson
Introduction by Charles Harold Herford

Print ISBN 13: 978-1-4209-5336-7
eBook ISBN 13: 978-1-4209-5337-4

Cover Image: A detail of 'With Bated Breath and Whispering Humbleness,' illustration from 'The Merchant of Venice,' c. 1910 (colour litho), Linton, James Dromgole (1840-1916) / Private Collection / Bridgeman Images.

Please visit *www.digireads.com*

CONTENTS

Preface

Registered at the Stationers' in July, 1598, but with a special proviso, "that it be not printed without license first had from the Right-Honourable the Lord Chamberlain." The theatrical company to which Shakespeare belonged were then known as "The Lord Chamberlain's Servants"; and the purpose of the proviso was to keep the play out of print till the company's permission were given through their patron. The play was entered again at the same place in October, 1600, his lordship's license having probably been obtained by that time. Accordingly two editions of it were published in the course of that year, one by James Roberts, the other by Thomas Heyes. These were evidently printed from two distinct manuscripts, both of which had probably been transcribed from the author's original copy. The play was never issued again, that we know of, till in the folio of 1623. The repetition of certain peculiarities shows it to have been there printed, with some alterations, from the quarto of Heyes.

The Merchant of Venice was also mentioned by Francis Meres in his *Wit's Treasury*, 1598. How long before that time the play was written we have no means of knowing; but, judging from the style, we cannot well assign the writing to a much earlier date; though there is some reason for thinking it may have been on the stage four years earlier; as Henslowe's *Diary* records *The Venetian Comedy* as having been originally acted in August, 1594. It is by no means certain, however, that this refers to Shakespeare's play; while the workmanship here shows such maturity and variety of power as argue against that supposal. It evinces, in a considerable degree, the easy, unlabouring freedom of conscious mastery; the persons being so entirely under the author's control, and subdued to his hand, that he seems to let them talk and act just as they have a mind to. Therewithal the style, throughout, is so even and sustained; the word and the character are so fitted to each other; the laws of dramatic proportion are so well observed; and the work is so free from any jarring or falling-out from the due course and order of art; as to justify the belief that the whole was written in same stage of intellectual growth and furnishing.

In the composition of this play the Poet drew largely from preceding writers. Novelty of plot or story there is almost none. Nevertheless, in conception and development of character, in poetical texture and grain, in sap and flavour of wit and humour, and in all that touches the real life and virtue of the workmanship, it is one of the most original productions that ever issued from the human mind. Of the materials here used, some were so much the common stock of European literature before the Poet's time, and had been run into so many variations, that it is not easy to say what sources he was most indebted to for them.

It is beyond question that there was an earlier play running more or less upon the same or similar incidents. For Stephen Gosson published, in 1579, a tract entitled *The School of Abuse*, in which he mentions a certain play as "The Jew, shown at the Bull, representing the greediness of worldly choosers, and the bloody minds of usurers." This would fairly infer that Shakespeare was not the first to combine, in dramatic form, the two incidents of the caskets and the pound of flesh: but, nothing further being now known touching the order and character of that older performance, we can affirm nothing as to how far he may have followed or used it in the composition of his play.

The original of the casket-lottery dates far back in the days of Mediaeval Romance; and the substance of it was variously repeated, from time to time, by successive authors, till Shakespeare spoilt it for further use. It is met with in the *Gesta Romanorum*, an old and curious collection of tales; and, as the version there given is clearly identified as the one used by Shakespeare directly or indirectly, it seems hardly worth the while to notice, here, any of the other versions.

Anselm, Emperor of Rome, having been long childless, has at length a son born to him. His great enemy, the King of Naples, wishing to end their strife, proposes a marriage between his daughter and the Emperor's son. The latter consents, and in due time the princess embarks for Rome. A terrible storm arising, the ship is wrecked, and all on board perish except the princess. Before she can make good her escape, she is swallowed by a huge whale. But she happens to be armed with a sharp knife, which she uses so vigorously in her strange lodging, that the whale soon has the worst of it. The monster thereupon makes for the shore, and is there killed by a knight, who rescues the princess, and takes her under his protection. On relating her story, she is conveyed to the Emperor, who, to prove whether she is worthy of his son, puts before her three vessels: the first made of pure gold, and outwardly set with rich gems, but within full of dead men's bones; the second made of fine silver, but filled with earth and worms; the third made of lead, but full within of precious stones. On the first is inscribed "Whoso chooseth me shall find what he deserveth"; on the second, "Whoso chooseth me shall find what his nature desireth"; on the third, "Whoso chooseth me shall find what God has disposed to him." The Emperor then orders her to choose one of the vessels, telling her that, if she chooses that which will profit herself and others, she shall have his son. The princess chooses the third, and is forthwith married to the young prince.

The incidents of the bond, the forfeiture, the pound of flesh, and the mode in which the penalty is escaped, are also related in the *Gesta Romanorum*, but not in connection with that of the caskets. It is certain, however, that in this the Poet did not draw from the *Gesta*, but, directly or indirectly, from an Italian novel, by Giovanni Fiorentino, written as early as 1378, though not printed till 1500. The main points of the story are as follows:

Giannetto, the adopted son of a Venetian merchant, Ansaldo, gets permission to visit Alexandria. On his voyage he lands at Belmont, where he finds a lady of great wealth and beauty, and falls deeply in love with her. He returns to Venice, asks for a supply of money to enable him to prosecute his love-suit, and Ansaldo borrows 10,000 ducats of a Jew on the condition that, if the money be not repaid by a certain day, Ansaldo shall forfeit a pound of his flesh, to be cut off by the Jew. Giannetto gains the lady in marriage; but, forgetful of the bond, prolongs his stay at Belmont till the day of payment is past. Hastening to Venice, he finds the Jew rigid in exacting the penalty, and not to be turned from it even by ten times the amount of the loan. The bride, knowing the merchant's position, disguises herself as a doctor of law, repairs to Venice, and gets herself introduced as a judge into the court where the case is on trial: for in Italy, at that time, nice and difficult points of law were determined, not by the ordinary judges, but by doctors of law from Padua, Bologna, and other famous law-schools. The lady, unrecognized by her husband, learns the nature of the case, and, after reading the bond, calls on the Jew to take the pound of flesh, but tells him he must take neither more nor less than exactly a pound, and that he must shed no blood. An executioner is at hand to behead him in case any blood be drawn. The Jew then says he will accept the 100,000 ducats offered; but, as he has declared up and down repeatedly that he will have nothing but the pound of flesh, the judge refuses to allow any repayment of money whatever; and the Jew in a rage tears up the bond and quits the court. Hereupon Giannetto, overjoyed at the happy issue, yields up to the judge, in token of his gratitude, a ring which his wife had given him on their marriage-day; and the judge, on returning home and putting off the disguise, rails at her husband in fine terms about his parting with the ring, which she says she is sure he must have given to some woman.

There is also an old ballad entitled "The cruelty of Gernutus, a Jew, who, lending to a Merchant a hundred crowns, would have a pound of his flesh, because he could not pay him at the day appointed." The ballad is of uncertain date; but Bishop Percy, who reprints it in his *Reliques* "from an ancient blackletter copy," justly infers it to have been earlier than the play, because "it differs from the play in many circumstances which a mere ballad-maker would hardly have given himself the trouble to alter." I subjoin so much of it as is pertinent to the occasion:

In Venice town, not long ago,
   A cruel Jew did dwell,
Which lived all on usury,
   As Italian writers tell.

Within that city dwelt that time
   A merchant of great fame,
Which, being distressed, in his need
   Unto Gernutus came;

Desiring him to stand his friend,
   For twelvemonth and a day
To lend to him an hundred crowns;
   And he for it would pay

Whatsoever he would demand of him;
   And pledges he should have.
No, quoth the Jew with fleering looks,
   Sir, ask what you will have.

No penny for the loan of it
   For one year you shall pay:
You may do me as good a turn,
   Before my dying day.

But we will have a merry jest
   For to be talked long:
You shall make me a bond, quoth he,
   That shall be large and strong.

And this shall be the forfeiture,—
   Of your own flesh a pound:
If you agree, make you the bond,
   And here is a hundred crowns.

With right good will! the merchant says;
   And so the bond was made.
When twelvemonth and a day drew on,
   That back it should be paid,

The merchant's ships were all at sea,
   And money came not in:
Which way to take, or what to do,
   To think he doth begin.

Some offer'd for his hundred crowns
    Five hundred for to pay;
And some a thousand, two, or three,
    Yet still he did denay.

And, at the last, ten thousand crowns
    They offer'd, him to save:
Gernutus said, I will no gold,—
    My forfeit I will have.

The bloody Jew now ready is,
    With whetted blade in hand,
To spoil the blood of innocent,
    By forfeit of his bond.

And, as he was about to strike
    In him the deadly blow,
Stay, quoth the judge, thy cruelty,—
    I charge thee to do so.

Sith needs thou wilt thy forfeit have,
    Which is of flesh a pound,
See that thou shed no drop of blood.
    Nor yet the man confound.

For, if thou do, like murderer
    Thou here shalt hanged be;
Likewise of flesh see that thou cut
    No more than 'longs to thee;

For if thou take either more or less,
    To the value of a mite,
Thou shalt be hanged presently,
    As is both law and right.

Gernutus now wax'd frantic mad,
    And wots not what to say;
Quoth he at last, Ten thousand crowns
    I will that he shall pay;

And so I grant to let him free.
The judge doth answer make,—
You shall not have a penny given:
Your forfeiture now take.

HENRY HUDSON

1881.

Introduction

Two Quarto editions of *The Merchant of Venice* were issued in 1600. The first (Q_1) was printed by James Roberts and issued in his own name. He had designed to publish it two years before, and entered it accordingly in the Stationers' Register (22nd July 1598) as '*A booke of the Merchaunt of Venyse, otherwise called the Jewe of Venise.*' The entry is followed, however, by a proviso 'that it be not printed by the said James Roberts or any other whatsoever without leave first had from the ryght honourable the Lord Chamberlan.' In 1600 this leave was apparently obtained, and Roberts issued his Quarto with the following title-page:—

The | excellent | History of the Mer | *chant of Venice.* | With the extreme cruelty of *Shylocke* | the Iew towards the saide Merchant, in cut- | *ting a iust pound of his flesh. And the obtaining* | of *Portia*, by the choyse of | *three Caskets* | Written by W. Shakespeare. | Printed by J. Roberts, 1600.

On 28th October, however, in the same year, another edition of the play was entered on the Register by Thomas Heyes, 'by consent of Master Robertes.' The title-page of this Quarto (Q_2) is as follows:—

The most excellent | Historie of the *Merchant* | *of Venice* | with the extreame crueltie of Shylocke the Jewe | towards the sayd Merchant, in cutting a iust pound | of his flesh: and the obtayning of *Portia* | by the choyse of three | chests. | *As it hath beene divers times acted by the Lord Chamberlaine his Servants.* | Written by William Shakespeare. At London. Printed by I. R. for Thomas Heyes.

This 'I. R.' was, then, probably Roberts, who, after issuing his own edition, seems to have printed a second for Heyes. Heyes's was afterwards used for the Folio. Neither of the two Quartos, however, was printed from the other. Their differences are on the whole trifling, but they have a few glaring errors in common, and were probably printed from different transcripts of a single copy of the author's MS. The second Quarto was reprinted in 1637 (Q_3) with a list of the actors' names, and again in 1652 (Q_4).

In spite of its great and sustained popularity in later times, the play is rarely alluded to in the seventeenth century. But we know that one of Burbadge's most famous roles was that of

the red-haired Jew,
Which sought the bankrupt merchant's pound of flesh.[1]

English comedians carried it to Germany, and some critics have suspected a rude adaptation of it in the *Komödie von einem König von Cypern und von einem Herzog von Venedig*, which John Green's company played in 1608 at the court of Graz in Steiermark,[2] and in other places. Nine years earlier, when Shakespeare's play had been on the boards some two or three, a curious Latin drama (*Moschus*, by Jacob Rosefeldt) on the bond story was acted at Jena (July 1599) in celebration of a professional wedding. It is quite credible that *The Merchant of Venice* should have been acted in Germany in 1597-98; but the *Moschus* treats the story in an independent though fresh and lively way, and can only be regarded as a parallel.[3]

The Merchant of Venice was, as has been said, entered by Roberts in the Stationers' Register in July 1598. It is mentioned by Meres in his *Palladis Tamia*, published the same autumn, as a well-known piece. Two passages are imitated in the poor play of *Wily Beguiled*, which is plausibly assigned to 1597.[4] Silvayn's *Orator*, translated in 1596, perhaps supplied suggestions for the trial-scene. External evidence supplies no further data. But the maturity of style and the extraordinary skill of the composition forbid us to place it very near even the ripest of the early comedies. It probably belongs to 1596-97.

All discussion of the origin of *The Merchant of Venice* has to reckon at the outset with a brief notice by Stephen Gosson of the lost play called *The Jew*. A converted player, bitterly hostile to the stage, he

---

[1] Elegy on Richard Burbadge (d. 13th March 1618).

[2] Meissner, *Die englischen Komödianten zur Zeit Shakespeare's in Österreich*, 1884, p. 127 f. (quoted by J. Bolte, *Jahrbuch*, xxi. 193). Meissner supposes this to be substantially preserved in the extant *Jud von Venetien*, which contains a rude transcript of the trial-scene. But Bolte has shown that this is probably later than the Thirty Years' War (*Jahrbuch*, xxii. 189 f.).

[3] Cf. the account of it by J. Bolte, the first living authority on the Humanist Latin drama, in *Jahrbuch*, xxi. 187 f. Bassanio and his wooing are wholly absent; Antonio ('Polyharpax') is a grasping merchant who himself proposes the bond in pure whim! He is saved by the intervention of his brother, an unworldly scholar who despises money-making and lives only for learning; and the moral of his triumph is duly brought home to the academic audience.

[4] The most palpable copy occurs in the dialogue of Sophos and Lelia:—

Soph. In such a night did Paris win his love.
Lel. In such a night Æneas prov'd unkind.
Soph. In such a night did Troilus court his dear, etc.

excepts from his general anathema some four plays as 'without rebuke': 'The two prose books played at the Belsavage, where you shall never find a word without wit, never a line without pith, never a letter placed in vaine. *The Jew*, and *Ptolone*, shown at the Bull: the one representing the greediness of worldly chusers, and bloody minds of usurers; the other, very lively, describing how seditious states . . . are overthrown; neither with amorous gesture wounding the eye, nor with slovenly talk hurting the ear of the chaste hearers.'[5]

This brief notice tells us exceedingly little; but just enough to preclude the assumption that the plot of the *Merchant* took shape essentially in Shakespeare's hands. The author of *The Jew*, we can hardly doubt, had already illustrated 'the bloody minds of usurers' by the story of the pound of flesh, and 'the greediness of worldly chusers' by some variant of the three caskets, and Gosson's approval makes it evident that both morals were driven unmistakably home. Versions of the ancient pound-of-flesh story (though without the Jew) and of the caskets story, had entered English literature a century before in the English *Gesta Romanorum*. In a form much nearer Shakespeare, the pound-of-flesh story had been told by the Italian novelist, Ser Giovanni Fiorentino, in his *Pecorone* (pr. 1558), as well as, probably, in the ballad of *Gernutus the Jew*.[6] In the novel, as in the play, it is the fascinations of a lady of Belmont which set the whole in motion. But she is a rapacious and crafty siren, who allures passing merchants to wager their ships that they will possess her person, and then drugs their possets. Giannetto tries his fortune among the rest, borrowing the means from his godfather, Ansaldo; twice he leaves his ship behind in the harbour of Belmont . The third time, warned by the waiting-maid, he refrains from the drug and wins his wager. But Ansaldo, to equip his final expedition, has been compelled to borrow from a Jew on the familiar condition. The news that the Jew has claimed his bond startles Giannetto from the delirium of wedded bliss. As in the play, the lady despatches him, with ample means, to redeem Ansaldo, follows him in disguise, undertakes Ansaldo's defence, saves him by the no-drop-of-blood plea, and begs Giannetto's ring as her only reward. The Jew forfeits his loan, but suffers no further punishment. The gay crosspurposes and explanations of Shakespeare's fifth Act follow, but the lady does not, like Portia, heighten the fun by hinting at familiarities of her own with the doctor.

But it is only in her later career that she recalls Portia at all. She is still the lady of a fairy tale, whose character changes when her secret is

---

[5] *School of Abuses*, 1579 (ed. Shakesp. Soc., p. 30).

[6] *A new song shewing the cruelty of Gernutus the Jew, who lending to a Marchant a hundred crowns, would have a pound of his Flesh, because he could not pay him at the day appointed.* Printed in Percy's *Reliques*. The date of the song is uncertain, but it would probably have recalled the play more closely had it not preceded it.

discovered; Odysseus withstands her arts, and Circe becomes the most benignant of goddesses. In the world of the *Midsummer*-Night's *Dream* such a transformation might have been natural; in the riper comic art of the *Merchant* fairydom, though by no means banished, is only admitted in disguise. The crude, undramatic conditions which she imposes on her suitors must in any case have disappeared under his treatment. But it is probable that the old playwright had already replaced them by another, not only free from moral offence, but aptly leading up to the exposure of the usurer with a parable against worldly greed. Stories of 'worldly chusers' who preferred a gold to a leaden or silver casket, and found it full of dead men's bones, were current in various forms. One, as already stated, was known from the English *Gesta Romanorum*, and contains, at least, the germ of Shakespeare's casket-story. It had been published in Robinson's translation in 1577, two years before Gosson described *The Jew*.

A king's daughter, betrothed to an emperor's son, is sent by sea to be married to him. After being wrecked and swallowed by a whale, she reaches land alone, is brought before the emperor, and claims his son's hand. To test her worth, he causes three caskets to be made, one of gold, filled with dead men's bones; one of silver, filled with earth and worms; one of lead, filled with gold. The first was inscribed: *Whoso chooseth me shall find that he deserveth*. The second, *Whoso chooseth me shall find that his nature desireth*. The third, *Whoso chooseth me shall find that God hath disposed to him*. The maiden, considering that she deserved little, that her desires were ill, and that 'God never disposeth any harm,' chooses the leaden casket and is married.

But a trace has been pointed out of another version in which the wrong choice was made, and by a *man*. In his romance *Mamillia* (1583), Robert Greene thus enlarges on the text that virtue is the highest excellence of woman: 'He which maketh choyce of bewty without vertue commits as much folly as Critius did, in choosing a golden boxe filled with rotten bones' (ed. Grosart, ii. 114). This story, which Greene cites as familiar, forms a valuable link.[7] So much of the groundwork of the *Merchant* may plausibly be held to have been laid in the old play.

The immense artistic transformation which Shakespeare wrought in his materials we cannot measure with precision; but it is certain that no previous drama is so alive in every line with Shakespearean quality; and much of what is most Shakespearean in it presupposes literary and social influences more recent than 1579. In particular, the intense and terrible vitality of the figure of Shylock, beside whom Portia herself has almost the effect of a glorious picture, announces clearly enough the

---

[7] E. Koppel, 'Beiträge zur Geschichte des elisabethanischen Dramas' (*Eng. Stud.* xvi. 372).

powerful impression made upon Shakespeare by the Jewish character as he saw it in contemporary English life, and by Marlowe's grandiose incarnation of all its Machiavellian ferocity in the *Jew of Malta*. His intimate feeling for Hebraic characteristics has often fortified the theory that Shakespeare had seen the Continent, or even Venice itself. But, as Mr. Lee has shown,[8] the law which had for centuries banished the Jew from the realm was in the later years of Elizabeth entirely ignored. The Government itself eagerly employed their technical knowledge,[9] Elizabeth and her Court confided in a Jewish doctor, needy London resorted to the Jewish money-lender, and the Jewish vendor of old clothes was already a typical figure of the London streets. The rapid rise of the general scale of living, the growth of luxury and social ambition in all classes, made what was still branded as 'usury' a social need, and the Jews who swarmed in the great mercantile centres of the Continent, above all in Venice, flocked to London to supply it.

The author of *The Three Ladies of London* (pr. 1584) significantly makes 'Usury,' sometime servant of 'old Lady Lucre of Venice,' pass over to seek service with her grand-daughter 'Lucre,' in London, having heard that

> England was such a place for Lucre to bide
> As was not in Europe and the whole world beside.[10]

It is curious that the actual Jewish usurer, Gerontus, who figures in this play, is so far from anticipating the Shylock-type that he freely resigns both interest and principal to prevent his debtor, a wily Christian merchant, from abjuring his Christianity! Early in the next century English usurers were said (Webster, *The White Devil*) to be more extortionate than Jewish,—like the Italianate Englishman, surpassing his master.

But this was not the normal temper; and a few years later the mild Jew, Gerontus, was utterly effaced in the popular imagination by the spectacle of the two monstrous Jewish criminals, Barabas and Lopez. Marlowe's play was inspired by no Christian fanaticism. His Humanist thirst for colossal passions and energies found in the fierce intensity of Jewish race-pride and race-hatred, as in Tamburlaine's thirst for conquest and Faustus's thirst for power, the making of a Titanic tragic figure; and he threw himself into the exposure of Barabas's crimes with a frenzied impetus which doubtless impaired the poetic grandeur of his work, but even heightened its inflammatory virulence. Some four years

---

[8] New Shakespeare Society, *Transactions*, 1888.

[9] Thus, a certain Joachim Gauntz, who spent the years 1589-91 in England, furnished the Government with information about new methods of smelting copperas (Lee, *u.s.*).

[10] Hazlitt, *Dodsley*, vol. vi. p. 268.

later Roderigo Lopez, the Queen's Jewish physician, was charged with being concerned in a Spanish plot to poison her.[11] He was probably innocent, but Essex did his utmost to bring the charge home. Witnesses were got to testify to it on the rack, 'where men enforced do speak anything,' as Portia, perhaps significantly, is made to say (iii. 2. 35); and, in fine, Lopez was put on his trial in February 1594, and hanged at Tyburn amid the yelling execrations of the mob, in May. How heavily the supposed crime of Lopez told to the disadvantage of Judaism at large is shown by the series of vindictively anti-Jewish plays which in the ensuing months filled the benches and the treasury of the London theatres. The old *Jew* of Gosson's day was revived, and, during the remainder of the year, shared with Marlowe's *Jew* the chief honours of the stage controlled by Philip Henslowe. In May, Marlowe's *Jew* was entered on the Stationers' Register (though not printed till 1633), as well as the Gernutus ballad on the bond story. New plays on Jews and usurers were in brisk demand; one such was probably the lost *Venetian Comedy*, which Henslowe enters as 'new' in August.[12] Under such conditions the great rival company was not likely to rest idle, and Shakespeare, before all things a man of his age, did not refrain from turning the temporary sensation into matter for all time.

Not, however, by any deliberate approach to modern tolerance and humanity. The deliberate strokes of Shakespeare, so far as we can trace them, tend rather to make the vengeance which finally overwhelms Shylock more severe, and its justice more apparent. The Jew of the novel is foiled, like Shylock, by the quibble about shedding no blood; but the law, having foiled him, is satisfied. His attempt to commit a crime under shelter of the forms of law has been met by a still more stringent application of them than his own; equity is secured, and the plaintiff loses his suit and retires. But to Shakespeare's ethical sense this solution was inadequate. The plaintiff had planned a crime; his proper place was at the bar, and there accordingly he is in effect transferred when, as he is bursting indignantly from the court, he is checked by Portia's 'Tarry, Jew, the law hath yet another hold on thee.' The statute which she proceeds to quote against the alien who plans the death of any citizen is apparently Shakespeare's invention; it puts forward for the plain understanding the real meaning of Shylock's act and the real ground of the technical quibble which foiled it. But it also demanded a harsher penalty, and the total loss of what he values more than life is only averted by a *soi-disant* exercise of Christian mercy, and that at the price of resigning his Jewish faith.

---

[11] Lopez's tragic story is told in full by Mr. Lee, *u.s.*

[12] *The Venetian Comedy* possibly a further *réchauffé* of the bond story; and this is still more likely in the case of *The Jew of Venice*, printed, as was by T. Dekker, in 1653. But there is no evidence that this was not composed after the *Merchant*.

But, severely as Shakespeare judged Shylock, he entered into his situation with a marvellous intimacy of understanding which the modern world has excusably mistaken for sympathy. Marlowe painted the crimes of his Barabas, apparently, with a fierce delight in their anarchic ferocity. But his sympathy does not make us acquainted with Barabas as we are acquainted with Shylock; we do not hear in his anger or in his agony, as we hear in Shylock's, the cry of 'the martyrdom which for eighteen centuries had been borne by a whole tortured people.' Nor is there any approach to the imaginative insight with which, in the opening scenes, Shakespeare pictures the intercourse of two communities which meet but never mingle—the rich, despised, indispensable alien and pariah, clinging with the fanatical tenacity of his race to his rights, his moneys, and his religion, and the aristocratic caste, generous, emancipated, splendid, profuse, and needy. Out of this wonderfully life-like work the fantastic fable of the bond story starts with illusive reality. The casket story, even more fabulous, is perhaps less artfully assimilated. Portia's fate belongs to faery. For all explanation we are put off with Nerissa's light assurance that Portia's father devised it on his deathbed, where 'good men have holy inspirations.' What Shakespeare meant by this fantastic addition to the bond story is a problem which cannot be avoided if he did add it, but loses much of its urgency if the casket episode already belonged to the old play. Certainly, the whole bent of his art in this drama suggests that he was trying to make somewhat reluctant fantastic materials plausible and veracious, not at all to reinforce them with other materials still more fantastic. The romantic quality is incompletely disguised rather than deliberately assumed. It is not necessary, then, to discover in the casket story a profound inner connection with the bond story, to regard them as variations on the theme of 'the vanity of appearances,' or 'the relation of man to possessions.' But it is not to be denied that Shakespeare has communicated to both stories a mental atmosphere charged with the sense of wealth. Different ways of regarding and using wealth enter largely into the psychology of every character. Antonio lends, Bassanio borrows, Portia gives, and Jessica conveys; but all handle it with an aristocratic magnificence. The play that pleased Gosson may be surmised to have exposed the 'worldly chusers' in the interest of Puritan asceticism and austerity; but there is no shadow of asceticism in Portia's disdain for Morocco, and the significance of Bassanio's choice lies less in his ignoring outward show (which he was far from doing), than in his being ready, for love's sake, to 'give and hazard all he hath.'

The Merchant of Venice, beyond any other of Shakespeare's plays, suggests both a genial relish for opulence (and we know that in these years he was making and spending abundantly) and a familiarity with a splendid and elegant society. Some motives and situations of the earlier comedies of courtly life, especially *The Two Gentlemen*, are repeated, but there is a wonderful advance in intimacy of knowledge as well as in ripeness of art. The critical review of Portia's lovers in i. 2. is obviously a reworking of the scene between Julia and Lucetta (*Two Gent.* i. 2.), but there the maid does the criticism, here the mistress—a change which makes the dialogue both more piquant and also, according to Elizabethan notions, more consistent with good manners.[13] And the whole episode of Jessica, gracefully interwoven as a third story with the fortunes of Shylock and Bassanio, is far less a story of passionate love than of the charm which the world of 'high living and high thinking,' where Portia moves supreme, exercises upon the susceptible child of an alien race. The elements of the situation were perhaps due to Marlowe; there is no trace of it in the novel, and we may surmise, from Gosson's approval, that no such amorous adventure as Jessica's elopement occurred in the old play. Barabas's daughter Abigail also loves a Christian, Don Mathias; but she is her father's accomplice, not his betrayer, and the most obvious verbal similitude, his 'O girl! O gold! O beauty! O my bliss!' is spoken in ecstasy, not in anguish. She is an unhappy instrument in his desperate game, forced to love where he chooses, and deprived of her lover when it is no longer convenient to keep him alive. Abigail is a pathetic figure, though her creator, in his orgies of crime and bloodshed, has no leisure to make her pathos eloquent. Shakespeare deprived Jessica of any such appeal. Shylock was to stand alone, in gaunt solitude, unloving and unloved. Even the beautiful intimacies of many an outwardly sordid and miserly Jewish home—a trait which can hardly have escaped Shakespeare—are denied him. His household, upheld by fear, crumbles to pieces, and the captive spirits of grace and laughter, the 'beautiful pagan' and the 'merry devil' who robbed her 'hell' of some taste of tediousness, fly to their proper abodes. The modern world cannot quite forgive Jessica for deserting her father, still less for taking his ducats; but Shakespeare easily condones these incidents of an emancipation to which she establishes her full right by the native ease with which she moves in the new world as if to the manner born—an adept in its splendid extravagance and in its light badinage, but quick to take the impress of its serious enthusiasms and its generous virtue. It is not for nothing that the most splendid burst of poetry in the play is addressed to Jessica's ear, and the loftiest tribute to Portia uttered by her lips.

CHARLES HAROLD HERFORD

1901.

---

[13] B. Wendell, *W. Shakespeare*, p. 148.

THE MERCHANT OF VENICE

DRAMATIS PERSONAE

THE DUKE OF VENICE
THE PRINCE OF MOROCCO, *suitor to Portia.*
THE PRINCE OF ARRAGON, *suitor to Portia.*
ANTONIO, *a merchant of Venice.*
BASSANIO, *his friend, suitor to Portia.*
SOLANIO, *friend to Antonio and Bassanio.*
SALERIO, *friend to Antonio and Bassanio.*
GRATIANO, *friend to Antonio and Bassanio.*
LORENZO, *in love with Jessica.*
SHYLOCK, *a rich Jew.*
TUBAL, *a Jew, his friend.*
LAUNCELOT GOBBO, *a clown, servant to Shylock.*
OLD GOBBO, *father to Launcelot.*
LEONARDO, *servant to Bassanio.*
BALTHASAR, *servant to Portia.*
STEPHANO, *servant to Portia.*
PORTIA, *a rich heiress.*
NERISSA, *her waiting-maid.*
JESSICA, *daughter to Shylock.*
Magnificoes of Venice, Officers of the Court of Justice, Gaoler,
    Servants, and other Attendants

ACT I.

SCENE I.

Venice. A street.

[*Enter* ANTONIO, SALERIO, *and* SOLANIO.]

ANTONIO. In sooth,[1] I know not why I am so sad:
It wearies me; you say it wearies you;
But how I caught it, found it, or came by it,[2]
What stuff 'tis made of, whereof it is born,
I am to learn;
And such a want-wit[3] sadness makes of me,
That I have much ado to know myself.
SALERIO. Your mind is tossing on the ocean;
There, where your argosies[4] with portly sail,—
Like signiors and rich burghers[5] on the flood,
Or, as it were, the pageants[6] of the sea,—
Do overpeer the petty traffickers,
That curtsy to them, do them reverence,
As they fly by them with their woven wings.
SOLANIO. Believe me, sir, had I such venture forth,[7]
The better part of my affections would

---

[1] "In *sooth*" is *truly* or in *truth. Soothsayer* is, properly, *truth-speaker*; formerly used of men supposed to be wise in forecasting things.

[2] To *come by* a thing is to *get possession of it*, to *acquire* it. So the phrase is much used in New England, or was, forty years ago.

[3] A *want-wit* is a *dunce, simpleton*, or *dunderhead. Wit* was continually used for *mind, judgment*, or *understanding.*

[4] *Argosies* are large ships either for merchandise or for war. The name was probably derived from the classical ship Argo, which carried Jason and the Argonauts in quest of the golden fleece.

[5] *Signior* is used by Shakespeare very much in the sense of *lord; signiory*, of *lordship*, meaning *dominion.* Thus, in *The Tempest*, i. 2, Prospero says of his dukedom, "Through all the *signiories* it was the first." *Burghers* are citizens. So, in *As You Like It*, ii. 1, the deer in the Forest of Arden, "poor dappled fools," are spoken of as "being native *burghers* of this desert city."

[6] *Pageants* were shows of various kinds, theatrical and others; from a word originally meaning, it is said, a high stage or scaffold. Pageants of great splendour, with gay barges and other paraphernalia, used to be held upon the Thames. Leicester had a grand pageant exhibited before Queen Elizabeth, on the water at Kenilworth-Castle, when she visited him there in 1575; described in Scott's *Kenilworth.*

[7] *Venture* is what is *risked*; exposed to "the peril of waters, winds, and rocks."—The Poet very often uses *forth* for *out.* So later in the scene: "To find the other *forth*" And elsewhere we have the phrases, "find his fellow *forth*" and "inquire you *forth*," and "hear this matter *forth.*"

Be with my hopes abroad. I should be still[8]
Plucking the grass, to know where sits the wind,
Peering in maps for ports and piers and roads;[9]
And every object that might make me fear
Misfortune to my ventures, out of doubt
Would make me sad.

SALERIO. My wind cooling my broth
Would blow me to an ague, when I thought
What harm a wind too great at sea might do.
I should not see the sandy hour-glass run,
But I should think of shallows and of flats,
And see my wealthy Andrew dock'd in sand,[10]
Vailing her high-top lower than her ribs
To kiss her burial.[11] Should I go to church
And see the holy edifice of stone,
And not bethink me straight of dangerous rocks,
Which touching but my gentle vessel's side,
Would scatter all her spices on the stream,
Enrobe the roaring waters with my silks,
And, in a word, but even now worth this,[12]
And now worth nothing? Shall I have the thought
To think on this, and shall I lack the thought
That such a thing bechanced would make me sad?
But tell not me; I know, Antonio
Is sad to think upon his merchandise.

ANTONIO. Believe me, no: I thank my fortune for it,
My ventures are not in one bottom[13] trusted,
Nor to one place; nor is my whole estate
Upon the fortune of this present year:
Therefore my merchandise makes me not sad.

SOLANIO. Why, then you are in love.

ANTONIO. Fie, fie!

SOLANIO. Not in love neither? Then let us say you are sad,
Because you are not merry: and 'twere as easy
For you to laugh and leap and say you are merry,
Because you are not sad. Now, by two-headed Janus,[14]

---

[8] Here, as often, *still* has the force of *always*, or *continually*.

[9] *Roads* are *anchorages*; places where ships *ride* at anchor safely.

[10] *Dock'd in sand* is *stranded.*—Italian ships were apt to be named from Andrea Doria, the great Genoese Admiral.

[11] To *vail* is to *lower*, to *let fall.*—The image is of a ship tilted over on one side, the other side up in the air, and the top-mast down in the sand.

[12] Here the actor may be supposed to make a gesture importing bulk or largeness. The Poet often leaves his meaning to be thus interpreted.

[13] *Bottom*, here, is a transport-ship or merchant-man.

Nature hath framed strange fellows in her time:
Some that will evermore peep through their eyes
And laugh like parrots at a bag-piper,
And other[15] of such vinegar aspect
That they'll not show their teeth in way of smile,
Though Nestor swear the jest be laughable.[16]
Here comes Bassanio, your most noble kinsman,
Gratiano and Lorenzo. Fare ye well:
We leave you now with better company.
SALERIO. I would have stay'd till I had made you merry,
If worthier friends had not prevented[17] me.
ANTONIO. Your worth is very dear in my regard.
I take it, your own business calls on you
And you embrace th' occasion to depart.

[*Enter* BASSANIO, LORENZO, *and* GRATIANO.]

SALERIO. Good morrow, my good lords.
BASSANIO. Good signiors both, when shall we laugh? say, when?
You grow exceeding strange:[18] must it be so?
SALERIO. We'll make our leisures to attend on yours.

[*Exeunt* SALERIO *and* SOLANIO.]

LORENZO. My Lord Bassanio, since you have found Antonio,
We two will leave you: but at dinner-time,
I pray you, have in mind where we must meet.
BASSANIO. I will not fail you.
GRATIANO. You look not well, Signior Antonio;
You have too much respect[19] upon the world:
They lose it that do buy it with much care:

---

[14] Janus, the old Latin Sun-god, who gave the name to the month of January, is here called *two-headed*, because he had two faces, one on either side of his head. There is also an allusion to certain antique two-faced images, one face being grave, the other merry, or a gloomy Saturn on one side, and a laughing Apollo on the other.

[15] *Other* for *others* was a very frequent usage, especially in antithetic connection with *some*, as in this instance.

[16] Nestor was the oldest and gravest of the Greek heroes in the Trojan war. The severest faces might justly laugh at what *he* should pronounce laughable.

[17] *Prevented*, in old language, is *anticipated*. To *prevent* is literally to *go before*. So in the Prayer-Book, 17th Sunday after Trinity: "That thy grace may always *prevent* and follow us."

[18] *Strange* for *estranged, distant,* or *stranger-like*. Repeatedly so.

[19] *Respect*, in Shakespeare, often means *consideration*, or *concern*. So in *King Lear*, i. 1; "Since that *respects* of fortune are his love, I shall not be his wife." And so in North's Plutarch: "The only *respect* that made them valiant was, that they hoped to have honour."

Believe me, you are marvellously changed.
ANTONIO. I hold the world but as the world, Gratiano;
A stage where every man must play a part,
And mine a sad one.
GRATIANO. Let me play the Fool:[20]
With mirth and laughter let old wrinkles come,
And let my liver rather heat with wine
Than my heart cool with mortifying groans.
Why should a man, whose blood is warm within,
Sit like his grandsire cut in alabaster?
Sleep when he wakes and creep into the jaundice
By being peevish? I tell thee what, Antonio,
(I love thee, and it is my love that speaks,)
There are a sort of men whose visages
Do cream and mantle like a standing pond,
And do a wilful stillness entertain,
With purpose to be dress'd in an opinion
Of wisdom, gravity, profound conceit,[21]
As who should say *I am Sir Oracle,*[22]
And when I ope my lips let no dog bark!
O my Antonio, I do know of these
That therefore only are reputed wise
For saying nothing; when, I am very sure,
If they should speak, would almost damn those ears,
Which, hearing them, would call their brothers fools.[23]
I'll tell thee more of this another time:
But fish not, with this melancholy bait,
For this fool gudgeon,[24] this opinion.—
Come, good Lorenzo.—Fare ye well awhile:
I'll end my exhortation after dinner.
LORENZO. Well, we will leave you then till dinner-time:

---

[20] To *play the Fool* is, in Gratiano's sense, to act the part of a jester, such as that of Touchstone in *As You Like It*, or the Clown in *Twelfth Night*.

[21] *Conceit* was used for *thought, conception, judgment,* or *understanding*; as also *opinion* for *reputation* or *character*.

[22] "As who should say" was a phrase in common use, meaning "as if any one should say," or "were saying."—A "Sir Oracle" is one who conceives himself to have oracular or prophetic wisdom; a *wiseacre*.

[23] Referring to the judgment pronounced in the Gospel against him who "says to his brother, Thou fool." The meaning, therefore, is, that if those who "only are reputed wise for saying nothing" should go to talking, they would be apt to damn their hearers, by provoking them to utter this reproach. A thing is often said to *do* that which it any way *causes to be done*. The Poet has many instances of such usage. So in *Hamlet*, iii. 4: "An act that *calls* virtue hypocrite."

[24] That is," Do not bait your hook with this melancholy to catch this worthless fish." *Gudgeon* was the name of a small fish very easily caught; and which none but *fools* would care to catch.

I must be one of these same dumb wise men,
For Gratiano never lets me speak.
GRATIANO. Well, keep me company but two years more,
Thou shalt not know the sound of thine own tongue.
ANTONIO. Farewell: I'll grow a talker for this gear.[25]
GRATIANO. Thanks, i'faith, for silence is only commendable
In a neat's tongue dried and a maid not vendible.[26]

[*Exeunt* GRATIANO *and* LORENZO.]

ANTONIO. Is that any thing now?
BASSANIO. Gratiano speaks an infinite deal of nothing, more than any
man in all Venice. His reasons are as two grains of wheat hid in
two bushels of chaff: you shall seek all day ere you find them, and
when you have them, they are not worth the search.
ANTONIO. Well, tell me now what lady is the same
To whom you swore a secret pilgrimage,
That you to-day promised to tell me of?
BASSANIO. 'Tis not unknown to you, Antonio,
How much I have disabled mine estate,
By something showing a more swelling port[27]
Than my faint means would grant continuance:
Nor do I now make moan to be abridged[28]
From such a noble rate; but my chief care
Is to come fairly off from the great debts
Wherein my time something too prodigal
Hath left me gaged.[29] To you, Antonio,
I owe the most, in money and in love,
And from your love I have a warranty
To unburden all my plots and purposes
How to get clear of all the debts I owe.
ANTONIO. I pray you, good Bassanio, let me know it;
And if it stand, as you yourself still do,
Within the eye of honour, be assured,
My purse, my person, my extremest means,

---

[25] *Gear* was often used of any business, matter, or affair in hand.

[26] Not good for the matrimonial market, unless she have the rare gift of silence to
recommend her, or to make up for the lack of other attractions.

[27] "A more *swelling port*" is a grander and more imposing *appearance, deportment,*
or out-fit. *Something* and *somewhat* were used indiscriminately. "A somewhat more
swelling port" is the meaning.—*Grant,* in the next line, seems to be used, like *give,* with
two accusatives.

[28] That is, *complain of being* abridged, or *curtailed.* Here, as often, the infinitive, *to
be,* is used gerundively, or like the Latin *gerund,* and so is equivalent to *of being.*

[29] Gaged is *pledged.* So in *Henry IV., Part 1,* i. 3: "That men of your nobility and
power did *gage* them both in an unjust behalf."

Lie all unlock'd to your occasions.

BASSANIO. In my school-days, when I had lost one shaft,
I shot his fellow of the self-same flight[30]
The self-same way with more advised[31] watch,
To find the other forth, and by adventuring both
I oft found both: I urge this childhood proof,[32]
Because what follows is pure innocence.
I owe you much, and, like a wilful youth,[33]
That which I owe is lost; but if you please
To shoot another arrow that self[34] way
Which you did shoot the first, I do not doubt,—
As I will watch the aim,—or to find both
Or bring your latter hazard back again
And thankfully rest debtor for the first.

ANTONIO. You know me well, and herein spend but time
To wind about my love with circumstance;[35]
And out of doubt you do me now more wrong
In making question of my uttermost
Than if you had made waste of all I have:
Then do but say to me what I should do
That in your knowledge may by me be done,
And I am prest[36] unto it: therefore, speak.

BASSANIO. In Belmont is a lady richly left;
And she is fair, and, fairer than that word,[37]
Of wondrous virtues: sometimes[38] from her eyes
I did receive fair speechless messages:
Her name is Portia, nothing undervalued[39]
To Cato's daughter, Brutus' Portia:
Nor is the wide world ignorant of her worth,

---

[30] Arrows were variously formed for different ranges. A shaft "of the self-same flight" was an arrow made for shooting the same distance.—*His* for *its*, which was not then an accepted word, though it was just creeping into use. It does not once occur in our English Bible as originally printed in 1611. Instead of *its*, *his* is commonly used.

[31] *Advised* is *deliberate, careful,* or *circumspect.*

[32] *Childhood proof* is *childish instance* or *experiment*; a method he had used when a child. So the Poet has "*childhood* innocence."

[33] A youth wilful, or *headstrong, in expense* is the meaning.

[34] *Self* for *same* or *self-same*; a frequent usage. So in *King Lear*, i. 1: "I'm made of that *self* metal as my sister."

[35] Here, as often, *circumstance* is *circumlocution,* or *talking round* a thing, instead of coming to the point at once.

[36] *Prest* is *prompt, ready*; from an old French word. Spenser has it repeatedly in the same sense. The Latin *præsto* is the origin of it.

[37] Meaning she is beautiful, and has what is better than beauty.

[38] *Sometimes* and *sometime* were used indifferently, and often, as here, in the sense of *formerly* or *former.*

[39] *Nothing undervalued* is *not at all inferior in value.* So, later in this play, we have "ten times *undervalued* to tried gold." And *nothing* as a strong negative is very frequent.

For the four winds blow in from every coast
Renowned suitors, and her sunny locks
Hang on her temples like a golden fleece;
Which makes her seat of Belmont Colchis' strand,
And many Jasons come in quest of her.
O my Antonio, had I but the means
To hold a rival place with one of them,[40]
I have a mind presages me such thrift,
That I should questionless be fortunate!
ANTONIO. Thou know'st that all my fortunes are at sea;
Neither have I money nor commodity[41]
To raise a present sum: therefore go forth;
Try what my credit can in Venice do:
That shall be rack'd, even to the uttermost,
To furnish thee to Belmont, to fair Portia.
Go, presently inquire, and so will I,
Where money is, and I no question make
To have it of my trust or for my sake. [*Exeunt.*]

SCENE II.

Belmont. A Room in PORTIA'*s House.*

[*Enter* PORTIA *and* NERISSA.]

PORTIA. By my troth,[42] Nerissa, my little body is aweary of this great world.
NERISSA. You would be, sweet madam, if your miseries were in the same abundance as your good fortunes are: and yet, for aught I see, they are as sick that surfeit with too much as they that starve with nothing. It is no mean happiness therefore, to be seated in the mean: superfluity comes sooner by white hairs,[43] but competency lives longer.
PORTIA. Good sentences,[44] and well pronounced.
NERISSA. They would be better, if well followed.
PORTIA. If to do were as easy as to know what were good to do, chapels had been churches and poor men's cottages princes'

---

[40] The language is awkward: "*as* one of them," we should say.
[41] *Commodity* is *merchandise*, any thing that might be pledged as security for a loan.
[42] *Troth* is merely an old form of *truth.*
[43] *Superfluity*, that is, one who is rich and fares sumptuously, sooner *acquires* white hairs, or grows old. See page 19, note 2.
[44] *Sentences* for *maxims*, or axiomatic sayings; like Milton's "brief, *sententious* precepts."

palaces. It is a good divine that follows his own instructions: I can easier teach twenty what were good to be done, than be one of the twenty to follow mine own teaching. The brain may devise laws for the blood;[45] but a hot temper leaps o'er a cold decree: such a hare is madness the youth, to skip o'er the meshes of good counsel the cripple. But this reasoning[46] is not in the fashion to choose me a husband. O me, the word *choose*! I may neither choose whom I would nor refuse whom I dislike; so is the will of a living daughter curb'd by the will[47] of a dead father. Is it not hard, Nerissa, that I cannot choose one nor refuse none?

NERISSA. Your father was ever virtuous; and holy[48] men at their death have good inspirations: therefore the lottery, that he hath devised in these three chests of gold, silver and lead,—whereof who chooses his meaning chooses you,—will, no doubt, never be chosen by any rightly but one who shall rightly love. But what warmth is there in your affection towards any of these princely suitors that are already come?

PORTIA. I pray thee, over-name them; and as thou namest them, I will describe them; and, according to my description, level at[49] my affection.

NERISSA. First, there is the Neapolitan prince.

PORTIA. Ay, that's a colt[50] indeed, for he doth nothing but talk of his horse; and he makes it a great appropriation[51] to his own good parts, that he can shoe him himself. I am much afeard my lady his mother played false with a smith.

NERISSA. Then there is the County Palatine.

PORTIA. He doth nothing but frown, as who should say, *An you will not have me, choose.* He hears merry tales and smiles not: I fear he will prove the weeping philosopher[52] when he grows old, being so full of unmannerly sadness in his youth. I had rather be married to

---

[45] *Blood* here means the same as *temper*, a little after; and both are put for *passion* or *impulse* generally.

[46] *Reasoning* for *talk* or *conversation*. The Poet repeatedly has *reason*, both as noun and verb, in the same sense.

[47] The second *will* stands for what we call "will and *testament*."

[48] The sense of *holy*, here, is explained by the words *virtuous and good; upright* and *true.* Often so.

[49] *Level at* is *guess* or *infer*. The Poet uses *aim* in the same sense.

[50] An equivoque on *colt*, which was used for a wild, dashing, skittish youngster. The Neapolitans were much noted for horsemanship.

[51] *Appropriation* is used rather oddly here,—in the sense, apparently, of *addition*. The word does not occur again in Shakespeare.

[52] This was Heraclitus of Ephesus, who became a complete recluse, and retreated to the mountains, where he lived on pot-herbs. He was called "the weeping philosopher" because he mourned over the follies of mankind, just as Democritus was called "the laughing philosopher" because he laughed at them. Perhaps Portia has in mind the precept, "*Rejoice* with those that do rejoice, and weep with them that weep."

a death's-head with a bone in his mouth than to either of these. God defend me from these two!

NERISSA. How say you by[53] the French lord, Monsieur Le Bon?

PORTIA. God made him, and therefore let him pass for a man. In truth, I know it is a sin to be a mocker: but, he! why, he hath a horse better than the Neapolitan's, a better bad habit of frowning than the Count Palatine; he is every man in no man; if a throstle sing, he falls straight a capering: he will fence[54] with his own shadow: if I should marry him, I should marry twenty husbands. If he would[55] despise me I would forgive him, for if he love me to madness, I shall never requite him.

NERISSA. What say you then to[56] Falconbridge, the young baron of England?

PORTIA. You know I say nothing to him, for he understands not me, nor I him: he hath neither Latin, French, nor Italian, and you will come into the court and swear that I have a poor pennyworth in the English. He is a proper[57] man's picture, but, alas, who can converse with a dumb-show?[58] How oddly he is suited! I think he bought his doublet in Italy, his round hose in France, his bonnet[59] in Germany and his behavior every where.

NERISSA. What think you of the Scottish lord, his neighbour?

PORTIA. That he hath a neighbourly charity in him, for he borrowed a box of the ear of the Englishman and swore he would pay him again when he was able: I think the Frenchman became his surety and sealed under for another.[60]

NERISSA. How like you the young German, the Duke of Saxony's nephew?

---

[53] "*What* say you *of* or *in reference to*?" *By* and *of* were often used indiscriminately. So in ii. 8, of this play: "That *many* may be meant *by* the fool multitude."

[54] To *fence* is to *manage the sword*; to practise the art of defence, as it is called. Skill in handling the sword was formerly an indispensable accomplishment of a gentleman.

[55] *Would* for *should*; the two being often used indiscriminately. So a little after: "You should refuse to perform."

[56] Here *to* is used like *by* in note 53. In the next speech, Portia plays upon the word, using it in the ordinary sense.

[57] *Proper* is *handsome* or *fine-looking*. Commonly so in the Poet's time. In Hebrews, xi. 23,the parents of Moses are said to have hidden him, "because they saw he was a *proper* child."

[58] A *dumb-show* is an action or character exhibited to the eye only; something like what we call a *tableau*.

[59] *Doublet* was the name of a man's outside upper garment.—*Hose* was used for *trousers* or *stockings*, or both in one.—*Bonnet* and hat were used indifferently for a man's head-dress.

[60] To *seal* was to *subscribe*; as Antonio afterwards says," I'll *seal* to such a bond." The principal sealed to a bond, his surety *sealed under*. The meaning therefore is, that the Frenchman became surety for another box of the ear, to be given in repayment of the first.

PORTIA. Very vilely in the morning, when he is sober, and most vilely in the afternoon, when he is drunk: when he is best, he is a little worse than a man, and when he is worst, he is little better than a beast. An[61] the worst fall that ever fell, I hope I shall make shift to go without him.

NERISSA. If he should offer to choose, and choose the right casket, you should refuse to perform your father's will, if you should refuse to accept him.

PORTIA. Therefore, for fear of the worst, I pray thee, set a deep glass of Rhenish wine on the contrary casket;[62] for if the devil be within and that temptation without, I know he will choose it. I will do any thing, Nerissa, ere I'll be married to a sponge.

NERISSA. You need not fear, lady, the having any of these lords: they have acquainted me with their determinations; which is, indeed, to return to their home and to trouble you with no more suit, unless you may be won by some other sort[63] than your father's imposition depending on the caskets.

PORTIA. If I live to be as old as Sibylla,[64] I will die as chaste as Diana, unless I be obtained by the manner of my father's will. I am glad this parcel of wooers are so reasonable, for there is not one among them but I dote on his very absence, and I pray God grant them a fair departure.

NERISSA. Do you not remember, lady, in your father's time, a Venetian, a scholar and a soldier, that came hither in company of the Marquis of Montferrat?

PORTIA. Yes, yes, it was Bassanio; as I think, he was so called.

NERISSA. True, madam: he, of all the men that ever my foolish eyes looked upon, was the best deserving a fair lady.

---

[61] *An* is an old equivalent for *if*. So used continually in Shakespeare's time. And so in the common phrase, "without any *ifs* or *ans*."

[62] The *wrong* casket. So in *King "John*," iv. 2: "Standing on slippers, which his nimble haste had falsely thrust upon *contrary* feet."

[63] *Sort* appears to be here used in the sense of *lot*; from the Latin *sors*. So in *Troilus and Cressida*, i. 3: "Let blockish Ajax draw the *sort* to fight with Hector."—"Your father's imposition" means the conditions imposed by your father.

[64] Shakespeare here turns the word *sibyl* into a proper name. That he knew it to be a generic, not an individual name, appears in Othello, iii. 4: "A sibyl, that had number'd in the world the Sun to course two hundred compasses, in her prophetic fury sew'd the work." Bacon, in his essay *Of Delays*, also uses the word as a proper name : "Fortune is like the market where, many times, if you can stay a little, the price will fall; and again, it is sometimes like *Sibylla's* offer, which at first offereth the commodity at the full, then consumeth part and part, and still holdeth up the price." The particular Sibyl referred to by Portia is probably the Cumæan Sibyl, so named from Cumæ in Italy, where she had her prophetic seat. Apollo fell in love with her, and offered to grant any request she might make. Her request was that she might live as many years as she held grains of sand in her hand. She forgot to ask for the continuance of her beauty also, and so had a rather hard bargain of it.

PORTIA. I remember him well, and I remember him worthy of thy praise.

[*Enter a* SERVINGMAN.]

How now! what news?

SERVINGMAN. The four[65] strangers seek for you, madam, to take their leave: and there is a forerunner come from a fifth, the Prince of Morocco, who brings word the prince his master will be here to-night.

PORTIA. If I could bid the fifth welcome with so good a heart as I can bid the other four farewell, I should be glad of his approach: if he have the condition[66] of a saint and the complexion of a devil, I had rather he should shrive[67] me than wive me.

Come, Nerissa.—Sirrah, go before.—

Whiles we shut the gates upon one wooer, another knocks at the door. [*Exeunt.*]

SCENE III.

Venice. A public place.

[*Enter* BASSANIO *and* SHYLOCK.]

SHYLOCK. Three thousand ducats,—well.[68]

BASSANIO. Ay, sir, for three months.

SHYLOCK. For three months,—well.

BASSANIO. For the which, as I told you, Antonio shall be bound.

SHYLOCK. Antonio shall become bound,—well.

BASSANIO. May you stead me?[69] will you pleasure me? shall I know your answer?

SHYLOCK. Three thousand ducats for three months and Antonio bound.

BASSANIO. Your answer to that.

SHYLOCK. Antonio is a good[70] man.

---

[65] An oversight, perhaps. There were *six* of them.

[66] *Condition* is *temper, disposition*. So used continually by Shakespeare, and other writers of his time.

[67] Devils were imagined and represented as of dark colour. So, in *Othello*, Iago says to Brabantio, "The Devil will make a grandsire of you," referring to the Moor's colour.—To *shrive* is to *absolve*; referring to the priestly act of confession and absolution.

[68] *Well* has here something of an interrogative force, and perhaps ought to be pointed interrogatively,—"Well?"

[69] Another instance of the indiscriminate use of words: *may* for *can* or *will*.—"*Stead* me" is *aid* me, or let me depend on you.

[70] Shylock means *good* in a business sense; of good *credit*.

BASSANIO. Have you heard any imputation to the contrary?

SHYLOCK. Ho! no, no, no, no: my meaning in saying he is a good man is to have you understand me that he is sufficient. Yet his means are in supposition: he hath an argosy bound to Tripolis, another to the Indies; I understand moreover, upon the Rialto, he hath a third at Mexico, a fourth for England, and other ventures he hath, squandered abroad.[71] But ships are but boards, sailors but men: there be land-rats and water-rats, water-thieves and land-thieves,—I mean pirates, and then there is the peril of waters, winds and rocks. The man is, notwithstanding, sufficient. Three thousand ducats;—I think I may take his bond.

BASSANIO. Be assured you may.

SHYLOCK. I will be assured I may; and, that I may be assured, I will bethink me. May I speak with Antonio?

BASSANIO. If it please you to dine with us.

SHYLOCK. Yes, to smell pork; to eat of the habitation which your prophet the Nazarite conjured the devil into.[72] I will buy with you, sell with you, talk with you, walk with you, and so following, but I will not eat with you, drink with you, nor pray with you. What news on the Rialto?—Who is he comes here?

[*Enter* ANTONIO.]

BASSANIO. This is Signior Antonio.

SHYLOCK. [*Aside.*] How like a fawning publican he looks!
I hate him for[73] he is a Christian,
But more for that in low simplicity
He lends out money gratis and brings down
The rate of usance[74] here with us in Venice.
If I can catch him once upon the hip,[75]

---

[71] *Squandered* here is simply *scattered, dispersed;* a usage of the time.

[72] Alluding to the permission given to the Legion of devils to enter into the herd of swine: St. Luke, viii. 33.—*Habitation* is used of the *body;* the dwelling-place, in this instance, of the devils.

[73] *For* was often used with the exact sense of our *because.*

[74] *Usance, usury,* and *interest* were all terms of precisely the same import in Shakespeare's time; there being then no such law or custom whereby *usury* has since come to mean the taking of interest above a certain rate. How the taking of interest, at whatever rate, was commonly esteemed, is shown in Lord Bacon's essay *Of Usury,* where he mentions the popular arguments against it: "That the usurer is the greatest Sabbath-breaker, because his plough goeth every Sunday; that the usurer breaketh the first law that was made for mankind after the fall, which was,' in the sweat of thy face shalt thou eat bread'; that *usurers should have orange-tawny bonnets because they do* Judaize; that it is against nature for money to beget money, and the like." The words in Italic show that usury was regarded as a badge of Judaism.

I will feed fat the ancient grudge I bear him.
He hates our sacred nation, and he rails,
Even there where merchants most do congregate,
On me, my bargains and my well-won thrift,
Which he calls interest. Cursed be my tribe,
If I forgive him!
BASSANIO. Shylock, do you hear?
SHYLOCK. I am debating of my present store,
And, by the near guess of my memory,
I cannot instantly raise up the gross
Of full three thousand ducats. What of that?
Tubal, a wealthy Hebrew of my tribe,
Will furnish me. But soft![76] how many months
Do you desire?—[*To* ANTONIO.] Rest you fair,[77] good signior;
Your worship was the last man in our mouths.
ANTONIO. Shylock, although I neither lend nor borrow
By taking nor by giving of excess,[78]
Yet, to supply the ripe wants of my friend,
I'll break a custom.—Is he yet possess'd[79]
How much ye would?
SHYLOCK. Ay, ay, three thousand ducats.
ANTONIO. And for three months.
SHYLOCK. I had forgot,—three months; you told me so.
Well then, your bond; and let me see,—But hear you:
Methought you said you neither lend nor borrow
Upon advantage.
ANTONIO. I do never use it.
SHYLOCK. When Jacob grazed his uncle Laban's sheep,—
This Jacob from our holy Abram was,
(As his wise mother wrought in his behalf)
The third[80] possessor; ay, he was the third,—
ANTONIO. And what of him? did he take interest?
SHYLOCK. No, not take interest, not, as you would say,

---

[75] Some explain this as a phrase of wrestling; others, of hunting. To *have one on the hip* was to have the advantage of him; as when a wrestler seized his antagonist by that part, or a hound a deer.

[76] *Soft!* is an old exclamative, meaning about the same as *hold! stay!* or *not too fast!* Often used by Shakespeare.

[77] That is, "may you continue well!" or, "good health to you!" So in *As You Like It*, v. 1: "God rest you merry!"—"Your *Worship*" was a common title of deference, meaning somewhat less than "your *Honour*" in the Poet's time.

[78] *Excess*, here, has the exact sense of *interest*. If one lends a hundred dollars for a year at six per cent, he takes six dollars in *excess* of the sum lent.

[79] *Possess'd* is *informed*; a frequent usage. So later in the play: "I have *possess'd* your Grace of what I purpose."

[80] The third, reckoning Abraham himself as the first. How Jacob's "wise mother wrought" is told in Genesis, xxvii.

Directly interest: mark what Jacob did.
When Laban and himself were compromised
That all the eanlings[81] which were streak'd and pied
Should fall as Jacob's hire, the ewes, being rank,
In the end of autumn turned to the rams,
And, when the work of generation was
Between these woolly breeders in the act,
The skilful shepherd peel'd me certain wands,
And, in the doing of the deed of kind,[82]
He stuck them up before the fulsome[83] ewes,
Who then conceiving did in eaning time
Fall parti-colour'd lambs, and those were Jacob's.
This was a way to thrive, and he was blest:
And thrift is blessing, if men steal it not.
ANTONIO. This was a venture, sir, that Jacob served for;
A thing not in his power to bring to pass,
But sway'd and fashion'd by the hand of Heaven.
Was this inserted[84] to make interest good?
Or is your gold and silver ewes and rams?
SHYLOCK. I cannot tell; I make it breed as fast:
But note me, signior.
ANTONIO. Mark you this, Bassanio,
The devil can cite Scripture for his purpose.
An evil soul producing holy witness
Is like a villain with a smiling cheek,
A goodly apple rotten at the heart:
O, what a goodly outside falsehood[85] hath!
SHYLOCK. Three thousand ducats,—'tis a good round sum.
Three months from twelve,—then, let me see; the rate—
ANTONIO. Well, Shylock, shall we be beholding[86] to you?
SHYLOCK. Signior Antonio, many a time and oft
In the Rialto,[87] you have rated me

---

[81] *Eanlings* are new-born lambs.—A *compromise* is a contract or mutual agreement.—See Genesis, xxx. 31-43.

[82] *Kind* in its radical sense of *nature*. The Poet has it repeatedly so. Also *kindly* for *natural*.

[83] The meaning of *fulsome* here appears from the words, "the ewes being *rank*." In Golding's Ovid, it is used of a sheep's *dugs*: "Whose *fulsome* dugs do yeeld sweete nectar."

[84] "Was this inserted *in Scripture?*" is the meaning, probably.

[85] *Falsehood* for *knavery*, as *truth* sometimes for *honesty*.

[86] Shakespeare always has *beholding*, the active form, in the sense of *beholden*, the passive. Of course it means *indebted*.

[87] In this scene we have already had "*on* the Rialto," and "*upon* the Rialto." Concerning the place meant, Rogers thus speaks in one of the notes to his poem on Italy: "Rialto is the name, not of the bridge, but of the island from which it is called; and the Venetians say *il ponte di Rialto*, as we say Westminster-bridge. In that island is the

About my moneys and my usances:
Still have I borne it with a patient shrug,
For sufferance is the badge of all our tribe.
You call me misbeliever, cut-throat dog,
And spit upon my Jewish gaberdine,[88]
And all for use of that which is mine own.
Well then, it now appears you need my help:
Go to,[89] then; you come to me, and you say
Shylock, we would have moneys: you say so;
You, that did void your rheum[90] upon my beard
And foot me as you spurn a stranger cur
Over your threshold: moneys is your suit
What should I say to you? Should I not say
*Hath a dog money? is it possible
A cur can lend three thousand ducats?* or
Shall I bend low and in a bondman's key,
With bated breath and whispering humbleness,
Say this,—
*Fair sir, you spit on me on Wednesday last;
You spurn'd me such a day; another time
You call'd me dog; and for these courtesies
I'll lend you thus much moneys?*
ANTONIO. I am as like to call thee so again,
To spit on thee again, to spurn thee too.
If thou wilt lend this money, lend it not
As to thy friend;—for when did friendship take
A breed[91] for barren metal of his friend?
But lend it rather to thine enemy,
Who, if he break,[92] thou mayst with better face
Exact the penalty.
SHYLOCK. Why, look you, how you storm!
I would be friends with you and have your love,
Forget the shames that you have stain'd me with,
Supply your present wants and take no doit[93]

---

exchange; and I have often walked there as on classic ground. In the days of Antonio and Bassanio it was second to none."

[88] *Gaberdine* was a long, coarse outer garment or frock. Caliban, in *The Tempest*, ii. 2, wears one big enough, it seems, to wrap both himself and Trinculo in.

[89] *Go to* is an old phrase of varying import, sometimes of reproach, sometimes of encouragement. *Hush up, come on, be off*, and *go ahead* are among its meanings.

[90] "*Eject* your *spittle.*" *Rheum* was used indifferently of what issues from the mouth, the nose, and the eyes.—*Spurn*, in the next line, is *kick*: the same as *foot*.

[91] *Breed*, here, is *interest*; that which is *bred* from the principal.

[92] This doubling of the subject, *who* and *he*, in relative clauses was common with all writers. Bacon has it very often. So in his *Advancement of Learning*: "*Which* though *it* be true, yet I forbear to note any deficiencies."

Of usance for my moneys, and you'll not hear me:
This is kind I offer.

BASSANIO. This were kindness.

SHYLOCK. This kindness will I show.
Go with me to a notary, seal me there
Your single bond; and, in a merry sport,
If you repay me not on such a day,
In such a place, such sum or sums as are
Express'd in the condition, let the forfeit
Be nominated for an equal pound
Of your fair flesh,[94] to be cut off and taken
In what part of your body pleaseth me.

ANTONIO. Content, i' faith: I'll seal to such a bond
And say there is much kindness in the Jew.

BASSANIO. You shall not seal to such a bond for me:
I'll rather dwell[95] in my necessity.

ANTONIO. Why, fear not, man; I will not forfeit it:
Within these two months, that's a month before
This bond expires, I do expect return
Of thrice three times the value of this bond.

SHYLOCK. O father Abram, what these Christians are,
Whose own hard dealings teaches them suspect
The thoughts of others!—Pray you, tell me this;
If he should break his day,[96] what should I gain
By the exaction of the forfeiture?
A pound of man's flesh taken from a man
Is not so estimable, profitable neither,
As flesh of muttons, beefs, or goats. I say,
To buy his favour, I extend this friendship:
If he will take it, so; if not, adieu;
And, for my love, I pray you wrong me not.

ANTONIO. Yes Shylock, I will seal unto this bond.

SHYLOCK. Then meet me forthwith at the notary's;
Give him direction for this merry bond,
And I will go and purse the ducats straight,
See to my house, left in the fearful guard[97]
Of an unthrifty knave, and presently

---

[93] *Doit* was a small Dutch coin, less in value than our cent.

[94] The language is odd, and rather obscure. The sense will come thus: "Let the *forfeiture* of a pound of your flesh be *named* or *specified* as an *equivalent* for the debt."

[95] *Dwell* here has the sense of *continue* or *abide.*

[96] To *break his day* was the current phrase for breach of contract.

[97] "*Fearful* guard" is a guard not to be trusted, or that gives cause of fear. To *fear* was used in an active as well as a passive sense. So in the next scene: "This aspect of mine hath *fear'd* the valiant."

I will be with you.
ANTONIO. Hie thee, gentle Jew.—[*Exit* SHYLOCK.]
The Hebrew will turn Christian: he grows kind.
BASSANIO. I like not fair terms and a villain's mind.
ANTONIO. Come on: in this there can be no dismay;
My ships come home a month before the day. [*Exeunt.*]

ACT II.

SCENE I.

Belmont. A Room in PORTIA's *House.*

[*Flourish of cornets. Enter the* PRINCE OF MOROCCO *and his train*; PORTIA, NERISSA, *and others attending.*]

MOROCCO. Mislike me not for my complexion,
The shadow'd livery of the burnish'd sun,
To whom I am a neighbour and near bred.
Bring me the fairest creature northward born,
Where Phoebus' fire scarce thaws the icicles,
And let us make incision for your love,
To prove whose blood is reddest,[98] his or mine.
I tell thee, lady, this aspect of mine
Hath fear'd[99] the valiant: by my love I swear
The best-regarded virgins of our clime
Have loved it too: I would not change this hue,
Except to steal your thoughts, my gentle queen.
PORTIA. In terms of choice I am not solely led
By nice direction of a maiden's eyes;[100]
Besides, the lottery of my destiny
Bars me the right of voluntary choosing:
But if my father had not scanted me
And hedged me by his wit, to yield myself
His wife who wins me by that means I told you,
Yourself, renowned prince, then stood as fair
As any comer I have look'd on yet
For my affection.

---

[98] *Red* blood is a traditionary sign of courage. Thus Macbeth calls his frightened servant a *lily-liver'd* boy; again, in this play, cowards are said to have *livers white as milk*; and an effeminate man is termed a *milksop*.

[99] Hath *frightened* or *terrified*. See last note of preceding scene.

[100] Portia means that reason and judgment have a voice potential in her matrimonial thoughts. So in *Hamlet*, iv. 3: "The distracted multitude, who like not in their *judgment*, but their *eyes*."—*Nice*, here, is *dainty* or *fastidious*.

MOROCCO. Even for that I thank you:
    Therefore, I pray you, lead me to the caskets
    To try my fortune. By this scimitar
    That slew the Sophy,[101] and a Persian prince
    That won three fields of Sultan Solyman,
    I would outstare the sternest eyes that look,
    Outbrave the heart most daring on the earth,
    Pluck the young sucking cubs from the she-bear,
    Yea, mock the lion when he roars for prey,
    To win thee, lady.—But, alas the while![102]
    If Hercules and Lichas play at dice
    Which is the better man,[103] the greater throw
    May turn by fortune from the weaker hand:
    So is Alcides beaten by his rage;
    And so may I, blind fortune leading me,
    Miss that which one unworthier may attain,
    And die with grieving.
PORTIA. You must take your chance,
    And either not attempt to choose at all
    Or swear before you choose, if you choose wrong
    Never to speak to lady afterward
    In way of marriage: therefore be advised.[104]
MOROCCO. Nor will not. Come, bring me unto my chance.
PORTIA. First, forward to the temple:[105] after dinner
    Your hazard shall be made.
MOROCCO. Good fortune then!
    To make me blest or cursed'st[106] among men.

    [*Cornets, and exeunt.*]

---

[101] "A History of the Wars between the Turks and Persians," translated from the Italian, was published in London in 1595; from which Shakespeare might have learned that "*Soffi*, an ancient word signifying a wise man," was "grown to be the common name of the Emperors of Persia." Ismael Sophi is said to have been the founder of what was called the Suffavian dynasty. The same potentate is twice referred to in *Twelfth Night.*— Solyman the Magnificent had an unfortunate campaign with the Persians in 1535.

[102] "Alas the while!" "Woe the while!" "Alack a day!" and "Woe worth the day!" were all phrases of the same or of similar import.

[103] If they try the question of which is the *braver* man by a game of dice.—Lichas was the servant or *page* of Hercules, who ignorantly brought to his master from Dejanira the poisoned shirt. Hercules was a descendant of Alceus, and so is called, in the Greek idiom, Alcides.

[104] *Advised*, again, for *cautious* or *considerate*. See page 24, note 31.

[105] That is, to the church, to take the oath mentioned just before, and described more particularly in the eighth scene of this Act. Bibles were not kept in private houses in the Poet's time; and such an oath had to be taken on the Bible.

[106] Here the force of the superlative in *cursed'st* retroacts on *blest*; so that the sense is *most blest or most cursed*. So in *Measure for Measure*, iv. 6: "The *generous* and *gravest* citizens."

SCENE II.

Venice. A Street.

[*Enter* LAUNCELOT.]

LAUNCELOT. Certainly my conscience will serve me to run from this Jew my master. The fiend is at mine elbow and tempts me saying to me *Gobbo, Launcelot Gobbo, good Launcelot,* or *good Gobbo,* or good Launcelot Gobbo, use your legs, take the start, run away. My conscience says *No; take heed,* honest Launcelot; take heed, honest Gobbo, or, as aforesaid, *honest Launcelot Gobbo; do not run; scorn running with thy heels.*[107] Well, the most courageous fiend bids me pack: *Via!*[108] says the fiend; *away!* says the fiend; *for the Heavens,*[109] *rouse up a brave mind,* says the fiend, *and run.* Well, my conscience, hanging about the neck of my heart, says very wisely to me *My honest friend Launcelot, being an honest man's son,* or rather an honest woman's son; for, indeed, my father did something smack, something grow to, he had a kind of taste; well, my conscience says *Launcelot, budge not. Budge,* says the fiend. *Budge not,* says my conscience. *Conscience,* say I, *you counsel well; Fiend,* say I, *you counsel well*: to be ruled by my conscience, I should stay with the Jew my master, who, God bless the mark, is a kind of devil; and, to run away from the Jew, I should be ruled by the fiend, who, saving your reverence,[110] is the devil himself. Certainly the Jew is the very devil incarnate; and, in my conscience, my conscience is but a kind of hard conscience, to offer to counsel me to stay with the Jew. The fiend gives the more

---

[107] To scorn a thing with the heels appears to have been an old phrase for spurning or kicking at a thing. Shakespeare has the phrase again in Much *Ado,* iii. 4. Launcelot seems to be in chase of a quibble between the heels as used in kicking, and the heels as used in running.

[108] "*Via!*" from the Italian, was much used as a sort of exclamatory imperative, meaning *away! ox go ahead!*

[109] *For the Heavens* was merely a petty oath. To make the fiend conjure Launcelot to do a thing for *Heaven's* sake, is a specimen of that "acute nonsense" which Barrow makes one of the species of wit.

[110] *Saving your reverence* is a sort of apologetic phrase for saying something coarse or profane; somewhat like our "If you will allow me to say so." "God save the mark" and "God bless the mark," are phrases of similar import. How the two latter grew into such use, or acquired such a meaning, is not very clear. But it appears that certain congenital *marks* on the person were regarded as ominous or ill-boding. So in *A Midsummer,* v. 1: "Never mole, hare-lip, nor scar, nor *mark prodigious,* shall upon their children be." And so the phrases appears to have meant, "May God avert the evil omen!" or, "May God render the token auspicious!"

friendly counsel: I will run, fiend; my heels are at your command; I will run.

[*Enter* Old GOBBO, *with a basket.*]

GOBBO. Master young man, you, I pray you, which is the way to master Jew's?

LAUNCELOT. [*Aside.*] O Heavens, this is my true-begotten father! who, being more than sand-blind,[111] high-gravel blind, knows me not: I will try confusions[112] with him.

GOBBO. Master young gentleman, I pray you, which is the way to master Jew's?

LAUNCELOT. Turn up on your right hand at the next turning, but, at the next turning of all, on your left; marry,[113] at the very next turning, turn of no hand, but turn down indirectly to the Jew's house.

GOBBO. By God's sonties,[114] 'twill be a hard way to hit. Can you tell me whether one Launcelot, that dwells with him, dwell with him or no?

LAUNCELOT. Talk you of young Master Launcelot?—[*Aside.*] Mark me now; now will I raise the waters.[115]—Talk you of young Master Launcelot?

GOBBO. No master,[116] sir, but a poor man's son: his father, though I say it, is an honest exceeding poor man and, God be thanked, well to live.[117]

LAUNCELOT. Well, let his father be what 'a will, we talk of young Master Launcelot.

GOBBO. Your worship's friend and Launcelot, sir.

---

[111] *Sand-blind* is *dim-sighted* or *purblind*. The origin of the word seems unknown: perhaps it is a corruption of *semi-blind*. Of course Launcelot makes it the turning-point of a quibble.

[112] To *try conclusions* is the old phrase for to *try experiments*. It is not quite clear whether Launcelot's *confusions* is a blunder for *conclusions*, or whether it is an intentional parody on the old phrase, by way of joke.

[113] *Marry* was continually used as a colloquial intensive, having the force of *verily*, *indeed*, or *forsooth*; like the Latin *heracle* and *edepol*. It grew from a custom of swearing by the Virgin Mary.

[114] *Sonties* is most likely a corruption either of *saints* or of *sanctity*. *Saunctes* is an old form of *saints*.

[115] Meaning much the same, apparently, as our phrase "to raise the *wind*"; that is, to make an opportunity, or breed a controversy.

[116] *Master*, which we have flattened into *mister*, formerly meant something as a title of respect. Shakespeare procured from the Heralds' College a coat-of-arms for his father, and had himself no right to be called *master* till he inherited the rank of gentleman thus conferred. Old Gobbo shrinks from giving his son the title, though he keeps calling him *master*, not knowing who he is.

[117] *Well to live* is an old phrase meaning the same as our *well off*. The old man is humorously made to contradict himself.

LAUNCELOT. But I pray you, *ergo*, old man, *ergo*, I beseech you, talk you of young Master Launcelot?

GOBBO. Of Launcelot, an't please your mastership.

LAUNCELOT. *Ergo*, Master Launcelot. Talk not of Master Launcelot, father; for the young gentleman, according to Fates and Destinies and such odd sayings, the Sisters Three and such branches of learning, is indeed deceased, or, as you would say in plain terms, gone to Heaven.

GOBBO. Marry, God forbid! the boy was the very staff of my age, my very prop.

LAUNCELOT. [*Aside.*] Do I look like a cudgel or a hovel-post, a staff or a prop?—Do you know me, father?

GOBBO. Alack the day, I know you not, young gentleman: but, I pray you, tell me, is my boy,—God rest his soul!—alive or dead?

LAUNCELOT. Do you not know me, father?[118]

GOBBO. Alack, sir, I am sand-blind; I know you not.

LAUNCELOT. Nay, indeed, if you had your eyes, you might fail of the knowing me: it is a wise father that knows his own child. Well, old man, I will tell you news of your son: [*Kneels, with his back to him.*] give me your blessing: truth will come to light; murder cannot be hid long; a man's son may, but at the length truth will out.

GOBBO. Pray you, sir, stand up: I am sure you are not Launcelot, my boy.

LAUNCELOT. Pray you, let's have no more fooling about it, but give me your blessing: I am Launcelot, your boy that was, your son that is, your child that shall be.[119]

GOBBO. I cannot think you are my son.

LAUNCELOT. I know not what I shall think of that: but I am Launcelot, the Jew's man, and I am sure Margery your wife is my mother.

GOBBO. Her name is Margery, indeed: I'll be sworn, if thou be Launcelot, thou art mine own flesh and blood. [*Taking hold of his back hair.*] Lord worshipped might he be! what a beard hast thou got! thou hast got more hair on thy chin than Dobbin my fill-horse[120] has on his tail.

---

[118] It was customary for young people to address any old man or woman as father or mother. Hence old Gobbo does not recognize his son on being called father by him. Shakespeare has other instances of the usage. So, in *King Lear*, Edgar, while leading the eyeless Gloster, addresses him repeatedly as *father*, without stirring any recognition, or even suspicion, of the relationship between them.

[119] Launcelot is overflowing with quirks, and here purposely inverts the order of his words. He probably means "your child that was, your boy that is, your son that shall be."

[120] *Fill-horse* is shaft-horse, or horse that goes in the *shafts*; *fill* being a common form of *thill*.

LAUNCELOT. [*Rising.*] It should seem, then, that Dobbin's tail grows backward: I am sure he had more hair of[121] his tail than I have of my face when I last saw him.

GOBBO. Lord, how art thou changed! How dost thou and thy master agree? I have brought him a present. How 'gree you now?

LAUNCELOT. Well, well: but, for mine own part, as I have set up my rest[122] to run away, so I will not rest till I have run some ground. My master's a very Jew: give him a present! give him a halter: I am famished in his service; you may tell every finger I have with my ribs. Father, I am glad you are come: give me your present to one Master Bassanio, who, indeed, gives rare new liveries: if I serve not him, I will run as far as God has any ground.[123]—O rare fortune! here comes the man: to him, father; for I am a Jew, if I serve the Jew any longer.

[*Enter* BASSANIO, *with* LEONARDO *and other* FOLLOWERS.]

BASSANIO. You may do so; but let it be so hasted that supper be ready at the farthest by five of the clock. See these letters delivered; put the liveries to making, and desire Gratiano to come anon to my lodging. [*Exit a* SERVANT.]

LAUNCELOT. To him, father.

GOBBO. God bless your worship!

BASSANIO. Gramercy![124] wouldst thou aught with me?

GOBBO. Here's my son, sir, a poor boy,—

LAUNCELOT. Not a poor boy, sir, but the rich Jew's man; that would, sir,—as my father shall specify—

GOBBO. He hath a great infection,[125] sir, as one would say, to serve,—

LAUNCELOT. Indeed, the short and the long is, I serve the Jew, and have a desire,—as my father shall specify—

GOBBO. His master and he—saving your worship's reverence—are scarce cater-cousins,[126]—

LAUNCELOT. To be brief, the very truth is that the Jew, having done me wrong, doth cause me,—as my father, being, I hope, an old man, shall frutify[127] unto you—

---

[121] *Of* and *on* were often used indiscriminately.

[122] To *set up one's rest* was a phrase in frequent use for to make up one's mind. Said to be taken from the old game of primero, where it meant a determination to stand upon the cards one had in his hand.

[123] In Venice proper it was not easy to find ground enough to run away upon. Not much surface there but water.

[124] *Much thanks!* from the French *grand merci.*

[125] *Infection* is an honest blunder, probably for *inclination.*

[126] Old Gobbo seems to mean that his son and Shylock are not very near kindred, or do not love each other much. *Cater* is, most likely, from the French *quatre.*

GOBBO. I have here a dish of doves[128] that I would bestow upon your worship, and my suit is,—

LAUNCELOT. In very brief, the suit is impertinent[129] to myself, as your worship shall know by this honest old man; and, though I say it, though old man, yet poor man, my father.

BASSANIO. One speak for both.—What would you?

LAUNCELOT. Serve you, sir.

GOBBO. That is the very defect[130] of the matter, sir.

BASSANIO. I know thee well; thou hast obtain'd thy suit:
Shylock thy master spoke with me this day,
And hath preferr'd thee,[131]—if it be preferment
To leave a rich Jew's service, to become
The follower of so poor a gentleman.

LAUNCELOT. The old proverb is very well parted between my master Shylock and you, sir: you have the grace of God, sir, and he hath enough.[132]

BASSANIO. Thou speak'st it well.—Go, father, with thy son.—
Take leave of thy old master and inquire
My lodging out.—[*To his* FOLLOWERS.] Give him a livery
More guarded[133] than his fellows': see it done.

LAUNCELOT. Father, in.—I cannot get a service, no; I have ne'er a tongue in my head.—Well, [*Looking on his palm.*] if any man in Italy have a fairer table which doth offer to swear upon a book, I shall have good fortune![134] Go to, here's a simple line of life![135] here's a small trifle of wives: alas, fifteen wives is nothing!

---

[127] *Frutify* is a Gobboism for *fructify*, which appears to have been a sort of cant term for *holding forth*; in speech, that is.

[128] Upon this passage, Mr. C. A. Brown furnishes the following: "A present thus given, and in our days too, and of doves, is not uncommon in Italy. I myself have partaken there, with due relish, in memory of poor old Gobbo, of a dish of doves, presented by the father of a servant."

[129] Another Gobboism for *pertinent* or *appertaining*.

[130] *Defect* for *effect*; another honest blunder.

[131] To *prefer* is, in old English, to *recommend*, and also to *promote*. Bassanio plays upon the two senses of the word.

[132] "He that hath the grace of God hath enough," or something such, appears to have been "the old proverb" in question. *Parted* is *divided*; and Bassanio is supposed to have the better half.

[133] That is, ornamented. *Guards* were trimmings, facings, or other ornaments, such as gold and silver lace.

[134] Launcelot, applauding himself for his success with Bassanio, and looking into the palm of his hand, which by fortune-tellers is called the *table*, breaks out into the reflection: "Well, if any man in Italy have a fairer table, which doth *not only* promise, *but* offer to swear upon a book, *that* I shall have good fortune."

[135] The line in the palm passing round the root of the thumb was called *the line of life*; that which begins near the root of the little finger, and extends towards the root of the fore-finger, was *the line of fortune*.

aleven[136] widows and nine maids is a simple coming-in for one
man: and then to 'scape drowning thrice, and to be in peril of my
life with the edge of a feather-bed,—here are simple 'scapes![137]
Well, if Fortune be a woman, she's a good wench for this gear.—
Father, come; I'll take my leave of the Jew in the twinkling of an
eye.

[*Exeunt* LAUNCELOT *and* OLD GOBBO.]

BASSANIO. I pray thee, good Leonardo, think on this:
   These things being bought and orderly bestow'd,
   Return in haste, for I do feast to-night
   My best-esteem'd acquaintance: hie thee, go.
LEONARDO. My best endeavours shall be done herein.

[*Enter* GRATIANO.]

GRATIANO. Where is your master?
LEONARDO. Yonder, sir, he walks. [*Exit.*]
GRATIANO. Signior Bassanio,—
BASSANIO. Gratiano!
GRATIANO. I have a suit to you.
BASSANIO. You have obtain'd it.
GRATIANO. You must not deny me: I must go with you to Belmont.
BASSANIO. Why then you must. But hear thee, Gratiano;
   Thou art too wild, too rude and bold of voice,—
   Parts that become thee happily enough
   And in such eyes as ours appear not faults;
   But where thou art not known, why, there they show
   Something too liberal.[138] Pray thee, take pain
   To allay with some cold drops of modesty
   Thy skipping spirit, lest through thy wild behavior
   I be misconstrued in the place I go to,
   And lose my hopes.
GRATIANO. Signior Bassanio, hear me:
   If I do not put on a sober habit,

---

[136] *Aleven*, says Dyce, is "a vulgarism (and archaism) for *eleven*,—formerly not
uncommon."

[137] Launcelot was an adept in the art of chiromancy, which in his time had its
learned professors and practitioners no less than astrology. In 1558 was put forth a book
by John Indagine, entitled "Brief introductions, both natural, pleasant, and also
delectable, unto the Art of Chiromancy, or manual divination, and Physiognomy: with
circumstances upon the faces of the Signs." "A simple line of life "written in the palm
was cause of exultation to wiser ones than young Gobbo. "The edge of a feather-bed" is
probably an absurd variation of the phrase "the edge of the sword."

[138] *Liberal* for *wanton, reckless*, or free beyond the bounds of decorum.

Talk with respect and swear but now and then,
Wear prayer-books in my pocket, look demurely,
Nay more, while grace is saying, hood mine eyes
Thus with my hat,[139] and sigh and say amen;
Use all the observance of civility,
Like one well studied in a sad ostent[140]
To please his grandam,—never trust me more.
BASSANIO. Well, we shall see your bearing.
GRATIANO. Nay, but I bar to-night: you shall not gauge[141] me
By what we do to-night.
BASSANIO. No, that were pity:
I would entreat you rather to put on
Your boldest suit of mirth, for we have friends
That purpose merriment. But fare you well:
I have some business.
GRATIANO. And I must to Lorenzo and the rest:
But we will visit you at supper-time. [*Exeunt.*]

SCENE III.

The Same. A Room in SHYLOCK's *House.*

[*Enter* JESSICA *and* LAUNCELOT.]

JESSICA. I am sorry thou wilt leave my father so:
Our house is hell, and thou, a merry devil,
Didst rob it of some taste of tediousness.
But fare thee well, there is a ducat for thee:
And, Launcelot, soon at[142] supper shalt thou see
Lorenzo, who is thy new master's guest:
Give him this letter; do it secretly;
And so farewell: I would not have my father
See me in talk with thee.
LAUNCELOT. Adieu; tears exhibit[143] my tongue. Most beautiful
pagan, most sweet Jew! if a Christian did not play the knave and
get thee, I am much deceived. But, adieu: these foolish drops do
something drown my manly spirit: adieu.

---

[139] People used to keep their hats on while eating dinner. While grace was saying,
they were expected to take the hat off and hold it over the eyes.

[140] That is, grave appearance; *show* of staid and serious behaviour. Os*tent* is very
commonly used for *show* among old dramatic writers.

[141] *Gauge* is *measure* or *estimate.—Bar* is *except.*

[142] *Soon at* is an old phrase for *about.* So in *The Comedy of Errors*, i. 2: "*Soon at*
five o'clock I'll meet with you upon the mart." Also in iii. 1: "And *soon at* supper-time
I'll visit you."

[143] *Exhibit* is a Gobboism for *inhibit;* that is, *prevent* or *restrain.*

JESSICA. Farewell, good Launcelot.—[*Exit* LAUNCELOT.]
    Alack, what heinous sin is it in me
    To be ashamed to be my father's child!
    But though I am a daughter to his blood,
    I am not to his manners.—O Lorenzo,
    If thou keep promise, I shall end this strife,—
    Become a Christian and thy loving wife! [*Exit.*]

SCENE IV.

The Same. A Street.

[*Enter* GRATIANO, LORENZO, SALERIO, *and* SOLANIO.]

LORENZO. Nay, we will slink away in supper-time,
    Disguise us at my lodging and return,
    All in an hour.
GRATIANO. We have not made good preparation.
SALERIO. We have not spoke us yet of torch-bearers.[144]
SOLANIO. 'Tis vile, unless it may be quaintly[145] order'd,
    And better in my mind not undertook.
LORENZO. 'Tis now but four o'clock: we have two hours
    To furnish us.—

[*Enter* LAUNCELOT, *with a letter.*]

    Friend Launcelot, what's the news?
LAUNCELOT. An it shall please you to break up this,[146] it shall seem
    to signify.
LORENZO. I know the hand: in faith, 'tis a fair hand;
    And whiter than the paper it writ on
    Is the fair hand that writ.
GRATIANO. Love-news, in faith.
LAUNCELOT. By your leave, sir.
LORENZO. Whither goest thou?
LAUNCELOT. Marry, sir, to bid my old master the Jew to sup to-night
    with my new master the Christian.
LORENZO. Hold here, take this: [*Giving money.*] tell gentle Jessica
    I will not fail her; speak it privately.
    Go. [*Exit* LAUNCELOT.]—Gentlemen,
    Will you prepare you for this masque tonight?

---

[144] Old language, meaning the same as *bespoken torch-bearers for us.*

[145] *Quaintly,* derived from the Latin *comptus,* was often used in the sense of *graceful, elegant,* or *ingenious.*

[146] *Break up* is old language for *break open.*

I am provided of[147] a torch-bearer.
SALERIO. Ay, marry, I'll be gone about it straight.
SOLANIO. And so will I.
LORENZO. Meet me and Gratiano
    At Gratiano's lodging some hour hence.
SALERIO. 'Tis good we do so. [*Exeunt* SALERIO *and* SOLANIO.]
GRATIANO. Was not that letter from fair Jessica?
LORENZO. I must needs tell thee all. She hath directed
    How I shall take her from her father's house,
    What gold and jewels she is furnish'd with,
    What page's suit she hath in readiness.
    If e'er the Jew her father come to Heaven,
    It will be for his gentle daughter's sake:
    And never dare misfortune cross her foot,
    Unless she do it under this excuse,—
    That she is issue to a faithless[148] Jew.
    Come, go with me; peruse this as thou goest:
    Fair Jessica shall be my torch-bearer. [*Exeunt.*]

SCENE V.

The Same. Before SHYLOCK's *House.*

[*Enter* SHYLOCK *and* LAUNCELOT.]

SHYLOCK. Well, thou shalt see, thy eyes shall be thy judge,
    The difference of old Shylock and Bassanio:—
    What, Jessica!—thou shalt not gormandise,
    As thou hast done with me,—what, Jessica!—
    And sleep and snore, and rend apparel out.—
    Why, Jessica, I say!
LAUNCELOT. Why, Jessica!
SHYLOCK. Who bids thee call? I do not bid thee call.
LAUNCELOT. Your worship was wont to tell me that I could do
    nothing without bidding.

[*Enter* JESSICA.]

JESSICA. Call you? what is your will?
SHYLOCK. I am bid forth to supper, Jessica:
    There are my keys. But wherefore should I go?

---

[147] The prepositions *of, with,* and *by,* were often used indifferently. So in Bacon's *Advancement of Learning:* "He is invested *of* a precedent disposition." See page 27, note 53.

[148] *Faithless* in the sense of *unbelieving,* or *without faith.*

I am not bid for love; they flatter me:
But yet I'll go in hate, to feed upon
The prodigal Christian.[149]—Jessica, my girl,
Look to my house.—I am right loath to go:
There is some ill a-brewing towards my rest,
For I did dream of money-bags to-night.[150]

LAUNCELOT. I beseech you, sir, go: my young master doth expect
your reproach.

SHYLOCK. So do I his.[151]

LAUNCELOT. An they have conspired together,—I will not say you
shall see a masque; but if you do, then it was not for nothing that
my nose fell a-bleeding on Black-Monday[152] last at six o'clock i'
the morning, falling out that year on Ash-Wednesday was four
year, in the afternoon.

SHYLOCK. What, are there masques?—Hear you me, Jessica:
Lock up my doors; and when you hear the drum
And the vile squealing of the wry-neck'd fife,[153]
Clamber not you up to the casements then,
Nor thrust your head into the public street
To gaze on Christian fools with varnish'd faces;[154]
But stop my house's ears,—I mean my casements:
Let not the sound of shallow foppery enter
My sober house.—By Jacob's staff,[155] I swear,
I have no mind of feasting forth to-night:
But I will go.—Go you before me, sirrah;
Say I will come.

---

[149] In i. 3, Shylock says, "I will *not eat* with you, drink with you, nor pray with
you." Did the Poet commit an oversight, or did he mean to put the Jew at odds with
himself out of hatred to the Christian?

[150] *To-night* here means what we call *last* night, or *the past* night.

[151] *Reproach* is a Gobboism for *approach*. Shylock chooses to take him in the sense
of *reproach*. And he expects Bassanio's reproach through the bankruptcy of Antonio.
This may have some bearing on the question whether Shylock has any hand in getting up
the reports of Antonio's "losses at sea."

[152] Easter-Monday. The origin of the name is thus explained by Stowe: "In the 34th
of Edward III., the 14th of April, and the morrow after Easterday, King Edward, with his
host, lay before the city of Paris: which day was full dark of mist and hail, and so bitter
cold, that many men died on their horses' backs with the cold. Wherefore unto this day it
hath been called *Black-Monday*."—*Bleeding at the nose* was anciently considered
ominous.—The closing part of the speech means *nonsense* merely.

[153] There has been some dispute whether *wry-neck'd fife* mean the instrument or the
musician. Boswell cited a passage from Barnabe Rich's *Aphorisms*, 1618, which appears
to settle the matter: "A *fife* is a *wry-neckt musician*, for he always looks away from his
instrument."

[154] Alluding perhaps to the painted masks; but meaning, withal, an insinuation of
duplicity, or doublefacedness.

[155] Hebrews, xi. 21: "By faith, Jacob, when he was a-dying, blessed both the sons of
Joseph; and worshipped, leaning upon the top of his staff."

LAUNCELOT. I will go before, sir.—
  Mistress, look out at window, for all this,
    There will come a Christian boy,
    Will be worth a Jewess' eye.[156] [*Exit.*]
SHYLOCK. What says that fool of Hagar's offspring, ha?
JESSICA. His words were *Farewell mistress*; nothing else.
SHYLOCK. The patch[157] is kind enough, but a huge feeder;
  Snail-slow in profit, and he sleeps by day
  More than the wild-cat: drones hive not with me;
  Therefore I part with him, and part with him
  To one that would have him help to waste
  His borrow'd purse.—Well, Jessica, go in;
  Perhaps I will return immediately:
  Do as I bid you; shut doors after you:
  Fast bind, fast find,—
  A proverb never stale in thrifty mind. [*Exit.*]
JESSICA. Farewell; and if my fortune be not crost,
  I have a father, you a daughter, lost. [*Exit.*]

  [*Enter* GRATIANO *and* SALERIO, *masked.*]

GRATIANO. This is the pent-house under which Lorenzo
  Desired us to make stand.
SALERIO. His hour is almost past.
GRATIANO. And it is marvel he out-dwells his hour,
  For lovers ever run before the clock.
SALERIO. O, ten times faster Venus' pigeons[158] fly
  To seal love's bonds new-made, than they are wont
  To keep obliged faith[159] unforfeited!
GRATIANO. That ever holds. Who riseth from a feast
  With that keen appetite that he sits down?
  Where is the horse that doth untread again
  His tedious measures with the unbated fire
  That he did pace them first? All things that are,
  Are with more spirit chased than enjoy'd.

---

[156] The worth of a Jew's eye was the price with which the Jews used to buy themselves off from mutilation. The expression became proverbial, and was kept up long after its original meaning was lost.

[157] This use of *patch* sprang from the motley or *patched* dress worn by professional Fools. Hence a general term of contempt. So in *A Midsummer-Night's Dream*, iii. 2: "A crew of *patches*, rude mechanicals, that work for bread upon Athenian stalls."

[158] Classic fable imagined Venus and her son Cupid to ride through the air in a chariot drawn by doves. So in *The Tempest*, iv. 1: "I met her deity cutting the clouds towards Paphos, and her son *dove-drawn* with her."

[159] "*Obliged* faith" is *plighted* faith, or faith made obligatory by solemn vows, as in marriage.

How like a younker[160] or a prodigal
The scarfed bark puts from her native bay,
Hugg'd and embraced by the strumpet wind!
How like the prodigal doth she return,
With over-weather'd ribs and ragged sails,
Lean, rent and beggar'd by the strumpet wind!
SALERIO. Here comes Lorenzo: more of this hereafter.

[*Enter* LORENZO.]

LORENZO. Sweet friends, your patience for my long abode;[161]
Not I, but my affairs, have made you wait:
When you shall please to play the thieves for wives,
I'll watch as long for you then. Approach;
Here dwells my father Jew.—Ho! who's within?

[*Enter* JESSICA, *above, in Boy's clothes.*]

JESSICA. Who are you? Tell me, for more certainty,
Albeit I'll swear that I do know your tongue.
LORENZO. Lorenzo, and thy love.
JESSICA. Lorenzo, certain, and my love indeed,
For who love I so much? And now who knows
But you, Lorenzo, whether I am yours?
LORENZO. Heaven and thy thoughts are witness that thou art.
JESSICA. Here, catch this casket; it is worth the pains.
I am glad 'tis night, you do not look on me,
For I am much ashamed of my exchange:[162]
But love is blind and lovers cannot see
The pretty follies that themselves commit;
For if they could, Cupid himself would blush
To see me thus transformed to a boy.
LORENZO. Descend, for you must be my torchbearer.
JESSICA. What, must I hold a candle to my shames?
They in themselves, good-sooth, are too-too light.[163]
Why, 'tis an office of discovery, love;
And I should be obscured.
LORENZO. So are you, sweet,
Even in the lovely garnish of a boy.[164]

---

[160] *Younker* meant a *youngster*, or a young *gallant.*
[161] "Long abode" is long *tarrying*, or long *delay.*
[162] Her *change* of dress; referring to her masculine attire.
[163] A pun implied of light in a material and a moral sense.
[164] Another pun. Jessica means that she ought to be hidden; Lorenzo that her brightness is disguised.

But come at once;
For the close[165] night doth play the runaway,
And we are stay'd for at Bassanio's feast.
JESSICA. I will make fast the doors, and gild myself
With some more ducats, and be with you straight.

[*Exit above.*]

GRATIANO. Now, by my hood, a Gentile,[166] and no Jew.
LORENZO. Beshrew me but[167] I love her heartily;
For she is wise, if I can judge of her,
And fair she is, if that mine eyes be true,
And true she is, as she hath proved herself,
And therefore, like herself, wise, fair and true,
Shall she be placed in my constant soul.—

[*Enter* JESSICA, *below.*]

What, art thou come?—On, gentlemen; away!
Our masquing mates by this time for us stay.

[*Exit with* JESSICA *and* SALERIO.]

[*Enter* ANTONIO.]

ANTONIO. Who's there?
GRATIANO. Signior Antonio!
ANTONIO. Fie, fie, Gratiano! where are all the rest?
'Tis nine o'clock: our friends all stay for you.
No masque to-night: the wind is come about;
Bassanio presently will go aboard:
I have sent twenty out to seek for you.
GRATIANO. I am glad on't: I desire no more delight
Than to be under sail and gone to-night. [*Exeunt.*]

---

[165] *Close* is *secret*, properly; here, what conceals or keeps dark.

[166] Gratiano is disguised with a mask, and in swearing by his hood he implies a likening of himself to a hooded monk swearing by his monastic character.—There is also a play on the word *gentile*, which signifies both a *heathen* and *one well-born.*

[167] Here *but* has the force of *if not;*—"Beshrew me *if I do not love* her." So in *Othello*, iii. 2: "Perdition catch my soul *but* I do love thee!" The exceptive *but*, as it is called; from *be out.—Beshrew me* is an old adjuration, equivalent to *confound me*, or *plague take me.*

SCENE VI.

Belmont. A Room in PORTIA'*s House.*

[*Flourish of cornets. Enter* PORTIA, *with the* PRINCE OF MOROCCO, *and their Trains.*]

PORTIA. Go draw aside the curtains and discover
    The several caskets to this noble Prince.—
    Now make your choice.
MOROCCO. The first, of gold, who this inscription bears,—
    Who chooseth me shall gain what many men desire;
    The second, silver, which this promise carries,—
    Who chooseth me shall get as much as he deserves;
    This third, dull lead, with warning all as blunt,—
    Who chooseth me must give and hazard all he hath.—
    How shall I know if I do choose the right?
PORTIA. The one of them contains my picture, prince:
    If you choose that, then I am yours withal.
MOROCCO. Some god direct my judgment! Let me see;
    I will survey the inscriptions back again.
    What says this leaden casket?
    Who chooseth me must give and hazard all he hath.
    Must give,—for what? for lead? hazard for lead?
    This casket threatens. Men that hazard all
    Do it in hope of fair advantages:
    A golden mind stoops not to shows of dross;
    I'll then nor give nor hazard aught for lead.
    What says the silver with her virgin hue?[168]
    Who chooseth me shall get as much as he deserves.
    As much as he deserves!—Pause there, Morocco,
    And weigh thy value with an even hand:
    If thou be'st rated by thy estimation,
    Thou dost deserve enough; and yet enough
    May not extend so far as to the lady:
    And yet to be afeard of my deserving
    Were but a weak disabling[169] of myself.
    As much as I deserve! Why, that's the lady:
    I do in birth deserve her, and in fortunes,
    In graces and in qualities of breeding;

---

[168] Alluding to the silver light of the Moon, or rather to the virgin Diana, who was the Moon-goddess of old mythology.

[169] *Disabling* here has the sense of *disparaging* or *depreciating.*

But more than these, in love I do deserve.
What if I stray'd no further, but chose here?
Let's see once more this saying graved in gold
Who chooseth me shall gain what many men desire.
Why, that's the lady; all the world desires her;
From the four corners of the earth they come,
To kiss this shrine,[170] this mortal-breathing saint:
The Hyrcanian deserts[171] and the vasty wilds
Of wide Arabia are as thoroughfares now
For princes to come view fair Portia:
The watery kingdom, whose ambitious head
Spits in the face of Heaven, is no bar
To stop the foreign spirits, but they come,
As o'er a brook, to see fair Portia.
One of these three contains her Heavenly picture.
Is't like that lead contains her? 'Twere damnation
To think so base a thought: it were too gross
To rib her cerecloth[172] in the obscure grave.
Or shall I think in silver she's immured,
Being ten times undervalued to tried gold?[173]
O sinful thought! Never so rich a gem
Was set in worse than gold. They have in England
A coin that bears the figure of an angel
Stamped in gold, but that's insculp'd upon;[174]
But here an angel in a golden bed
Lies all within.—Deliver me the key:
Here do I choose, and thrive I as I may!
PORTIA. There, take it, prince; and if my form lie there,
Then I am yours. [*He opens the golden casket.*]

---

[170] Christians often made long pilgrimages to kiss the shrine of a saint, that is, the place where a saint's bones were enshrined. And Portia, because she enshrines so much excellence, though still but "a traveller between life and death," is compared to such a hallowed shrine. *Shrine*, however, was sometimes used for *statue*, and so it may be here.

[171] A wilderness of indefinite extent south of the Caspian Sea.—*Vasty* is *waste*, *desolate*, or *void*. So Bacon has the noun in his *Advancement of learning*: "Their excursions into the limits of physical causes have bred a *vastness* and solitude in that tract."

[172] That is, lead were unworthy even to enclose her cerements, or her Oi shall I think in silver she's immured shroud. The Poet elsewhere has *rib* in the sense of *enclose* or *protect*: in *Cymbeline*, iii. 1, he speaks of England as "Neptune's park, *ribbed* and paled in with rocks unscaleable and roaring waters."

[173] This is said to have been just the ratio of silver and gold in 1600. Now it is less than as one to sixteen.—*Undervalued* is *inferior in value*. See page 24, note 39.

[174] *Insculp'd upon* is *carved* or *engraved on the outside*.—The *angel* was so called from its having on one side a figure of Michael piercing the dragon. It is said to have been worth about ten shillings. Shakespeare has many punning allusions to it; as in *The Merry Wives*, i. 3: "She has all the rule of her husband's purse; he hath *legions of angels*?

MOROCCO. O Hell! what have we here?
A carrion Death,[175] within whose empty eye
There is a written scroll! I'll read the writing.

[*Reads.*]

> *All that glitters is not gold,—*
> *Often have you heard that told:*
> *Many a man his life hath sold*
> *But my outside to behold:*
> *Gilded tombs do worms enfold.*
> *Had you been as wise as bold,*
> *Young in limbs, in judgment old,*
> *Your answer had not been inscroll'd:*
> *Fare you well; your suit is cold.*[176]

Cold, indeed; and labour lost:
Then, farewell, heat, and welcome, frost!
Portia, adieu. I have too grieved a heart
To take a tedious leave: thus losers part.[177]

[*Exit with his Train. Cornets.*]

PORTIA. A gentle riddance.—Draw the curtains, go:
Let all of his complexion choose me so. [*Exeunt.*]

SCENE VII.

Venice. A Street.

[*Enter* SALERIO *and* SOLANIO.]

SALERIO. Why, man, I saw Bassanio under sail:
With him is Gratiano gone along;
And in their ship I am sure Lorenzo is not.
SOLANIO. The villain Jew with outcries raised the duke,
Who went with him to search Bassanio's ship.
SALERIO. He came too late, the ship was under sail:
But there the duke was given to understand
That in a gondola[178] were seen together

---

[175] A human skull from which the flesh has all decayed.
[176] His courtship, which had been made warm by hope, is now chilled and frozen by an entire and hopeless failure.
[177] *Part* for *depart*. So the word was frequently used.

Lorenzo and his amorous Jessica:
Besides, Antonio certified the duke
They were not with Bassanio in his ship.
SOLANIO. I never heard a passion[179] so confused,
So strange, outrageous, and so variable,
As the dog Jew did utter in the streets:
My daughter! O my ducats! O my daughter!
Fled with a Christian! O my Christian ducats!—
Justice! the law! my ducats, and my daughter!
A sealed bag, two sealed bags of ducats,
Of double ducats, stolen from me by my daughter!
And jewels,—two stones, two rich and precious stones,
Stolen by my daughter!—Justice! find the girl;
She hath the stones upon her, and the ducats.
SALERIO. Why, all the boys in Venice follow him,
Crying,—his stones, his daughter, and his ducats.
SOLANIO. Let good Antonio look he keep his day,
Or he shall pay for this.
SALERIO. Marry, well remember'd.
I reason'd[180] with a Frenchman yesterday,
Who told me, in the narrow seas that part
The French and English, there miscarried
A vessel of our country richly fraught:[181]
I thought upon Antonio when he told me;
And wish'd in silence that it were not his.
SOLANIO. You were best to tell Antonio what you hear;
Yet do not suddenly, for it may grieve him.
SALERIO. A kinder gentleman treads not the earth.
I saw Bassanio and Antonio part:
Bassanio told him he would make some speed
Of his return: he answer'd, *Do not so*;
Slubber[182] *not business for my sake, Bassanio*
But stay the very riping of the time;
And for the Jew's bond which he hath of me,
Let it not enter in your mind of love:[183]

---

[178] *Gondola* is the name of the vehicles in which people ride through the liquid streets of Venice. In Shakespeare's time Venice was the common resort of all who went abroad to see the world; as much so, perhaps, as Paris is now: so that to "have swam in a gondola" was a common phrase for having travelled.

[179] *Passion* for *passionate outcry*; the cause for the effect.

[180] *Reason*, again, in its old sense of *converse*. See page 26, note 46.

[181] *Fraught* for *freighted*. The Poet has it repeatedly so; and many other such shortened preterites.

[182] To *slubber* is to do a thing carelessly. So in Fuller's *Worthies of Yorkshire*: "Slightly *slubbering* it over, doing something for show, and nothing to purpose."

Be merry, and employ your chiefest thoughts
To courtship and such fair ostents of love
As shall conveniently[184] *become you there*:
And even there, his eye being big with tears,
Turning his face, he put his hand behind him,
And with affection wondrous sensible[185]
He wrung Bassanio's hand; and so they parted.
SOLANIO. I think he only loves the world for him.
I pray thee, let us go and find him out
And quicken his embraced heaviness[186]
With some delight or other.
SALERIO. Do we so. [*Exeunt.*]

SCENE VIII.

Belmont. A Room in PORTIA'*s House.*

[*Enter* NERISSA *with a* SERVANT.]

NERISSA. Quick, quick, I pray thee; draw the curtain straight:
The Prince of Arragon hath ta'en his oath,
And comes to his election presently.

[*Flourish of Cornets. Enter the* PRINCE OF ARRAGON,
PORTIA, *and their trains.*]

PORTIA. Behold, there stand the caskets, noble prince:
If you choose that wherein I am contain'd,
Straight shall our nuptial rites be solemnized:
But if you fail, without more speech, my lord,
You must be gone from hence immediately.
ARRAGON. I am enjoin'd by oath to observe three things:
First, never to unfold to any one
Which casket 'twas I chose; next, if I fail
Of the right casket, never in my life
To woo a maid in way of marriage: Lastly,
If I do fail in fortune of my choice,
Immediately to leave you and be gone.
PORTIA. To these injunctions every one doth swear

---

[183] *Mind of love* probably means *loving mind,* or *mind full of love.* The Poet
elsewhere has *mind of honour* for *honourable mind.*
[184] *Conveniently* is *properly* or *fittingly.*—*Ostents* for *shows* or *manifestations.* See
page 43, note 140.
[185] *Sensible* for *sensitive* or *tender.* The Poet has it repeatedly so.
[186] That is, *enliven* the *sadness* which he *clings to* or *cherishes.*

That comes to hazard for my worthless self.
ARRAGON. And so have I address'd'd[187] me. Fortune now
To my heart's hope!—Gold; silver; and base lead.
Who chooseth me must give and hazard all he hath.
You shall look fairer, ere I give or hazard.
What says the golden chest? ha! let me see:
Who chooseth me shall gain what many men desire.
What many men desire! that *many* may be meant
By[188] the fool multitude, that choose by show,
Not learning more than the fond[189] eye doth teach;
Which pries not to the interior, but, like the martlet,
Builds in the weather on the outward wall,
Even in the force and road of casualty.[190]
I will not choose what many men desire,
Because I will not jump[191] with common spirits
And rank me with the barbarous multitudes.
Why, then to thee, thou silver treasure-house;
Tell me once more what title thou dost bear:
Who chooseth me shall get as much as he deserves:
And well said too; for who shall go about
To cozen fortune and be honourable
Without the stamp of merit? Let none presume
To wear an undeserved dignity.
O, that estates, degrees and offices
Were not derived corruptly, and that clear honour
Were purchased by the merit of the wearer!
How many then should cover that stand bare![192]
How many be commanded that command!
How much low peasantry would then be glean'd
From the true seed of honour! and how much honour
Pick'd from the chaff and ruin[193] of the times
To be new-varnish'd! Well, but to my choice:
Who chooseth me shall get as much as he deserves.
I will assume desert.—Give me a key for this,

---

[187] *Address'd* is *prepared* or *made ready*; a common usage of the time. So in *The Winter's Tale*, iv. 4: "*Address* yourself to entertain them sprightly."

[188] *By*, again, where we should use *of*. See page 27, note 53.

[189] Here, as commonly in Shakespeare, *fond* is *foolish*.

[190] Where it is exposed to every accident or mischance.

[191] *Jump* for *agree*. So in *The Taming of the Shrew*, i. 1: "Both our inventions meet and *jump* in one." And in *1 Henry the Fourth*, i. 2: "Well, Hal, well; and in some sort it *jumps* with my humour."

[192] "How many then *would keep their hats on*, who now stand *bareheaded* as before their masters or superiors." Another instance of the indiscriminate use of *should* and *would*.

[193] *Ruin* here means *refuse* or *rubbish*.

And instantly unlock my fortunes here.

[*He opens the silver casket.*]

PORTIA. Too long a pause for that which you find there.
ARRAGON. What's here? the portrait of a blinking idiot,
Presenting me a schedule! I will read it.
How much unlike art thou to Portia!
How much unlike my hopes and my deservings!
Who chooseth me shall have as much as he deserves.
Did I deserve no more than a fool's head?
Is that my prize? are my deserts no better?
PORTIA. To offend, and judge, are distinct offices
And of opposed natures.[194]
ARRAGON. What is here?

[*Reads.*]

> *The fire seven times tried this:*
> *Seven times tried that judgment is,*
> *That did never choose amiss.*
> *Some there be that shadows kiss;*
> *Such have but a shadow's bliss:*
> *There be fools alive, I wis,*[195]
> *Silver'd o'er, and so was this.*[196]
> *Take what wife you will to bed,*[197]
> *I will ever be your head:*[198]
> *So be gone: you are sped.*[199]

Still more fool I shall appear
By the time I linger here
With one fool's head I came to woo,
But I go away with two.

---

[194] Portia is something of a lawyer, and she here has in mind the old legal axiom, that no man is a good judge in his own case.

[195] To *wis* is to *think*, to *suppose*. Nares derives it from the Saxon *wissan*. The preterite occurs in St. Luke, ii. 49: "*Wist* ye not that I must be about my Father's business?"

[196] The idiot's portrait was enclosed in the *silver* casket, and in that sense was *silver'd o'er.*

[197] An apparent oversight of the Poet's: the Prince was sworn "never to woo a maid in way of marriage." Perhaps, though, he might woo and marry a *widow.*

[198] "You will always have a fool's head, whether married or not."

[199] That is, "your case is decided, or *done for.*" So, in *Romeo and Juliet,* iii. 1, Mercutio, when he has received his death-wound from Tybalt, exclaims, "A plague o' both your Houses! I am *sped.*"

> Sweet, adieu. I'll keep my oath,
> Patiently to bear my wroth.[200]

[Exeunt with his train.]

PORTIA. Thus hath the candle singed the moth.
O, these deliberate fools! when they do choose,
They have the wisdom by their wit to lose.
NERISSA. The ancient saying is no heresy,—
Hanging and wiving goes by destiny.
PORTIA. Come, draw the curtain, Nerissa.

[Enter a SERVANT.]

SERVANT. Where is my lady?
PORTIA. Here: what would my lord?[201]
SERVANT. Madam, there is alighted at your gate
A young Venetian, one that comes before
To signify the approaching of his lord;
From whom he bringeth sensible regreets,[202]
To wit, besides commends and courteous breath,
Gifts of rich value. Yet I have not seen
So likely an ambassador of love:
A day in April never came so sweet,
To show how costly summer was at hand,
As this fore-spurrer comes before his lord.
PORTIA. No more, I pray thee: I am half afeard
Thou wilt say anon he is some kin to thee,
Thou spend'st such high-day[203] wit in praising him.—
Come, come, Nerissa; for I long to see
Quick Cupid's post that comes so mannerly.
NERISSA. Bassanio, lord Love, if thy will it be! *[Exeunt.]*

---

[200] *Wroth* is used in some of the old writers for *suffering*. So in Chapman's *22d Iliad*: "Born all to *wroth* of woe and labour." The original meaning of *wrath* is pain, grief, anger, any thing that makes one *writhe*; and the text exemplifies a common form of speech, putting the effect for the cause.

[201] A sportive reply to the Servant's "Where is *my lady*?" So, in *Henry IV., Part 1*, ii. 4, the Hostess says to Prince Henry, "O Jesu! *my lord*, the Prince!" and he replies, "How now, *my lady*, the hostess!"

[202] *Sensible regreets* are *feeling salutations*; or salutations that may be felt, such as valuable presents. See page 54, note 185.

[203] *High-day* is *holiday*; a time for finely-phrased speaking. So our Fourth of July is a high day; and we all know what Fourth-of-July eloquence is.

ACT III.

SCENE I.

Venice. A Street.

[*Enter* SOLANIO *and* SALERIO.]

SOLANIO. Now, what news on the Rialto?

SALERIO. Why, yet it lives there uncheck'd that Antonio hath a ship of rich lading wrecked on the narrow seas; the Goodwins,[204] I think they call the place; a very dangerous flat and fatal, where the carcasses of many a tall ship lie buried, as they say, if my gossip Report be an honest woman of[205] her word.

SOLANIO. I would she were as lying a gossip in that as ever knapp'd[206] ginger or made her neighbours believe she wept for the death of a third husband.[207] But it is true, without any slips of prolixity or crossing the plain highway of talk, that the good Antonio, the honest Antonio,—O that I had a title good enough to keep his name company!—

SALERIO. Come, the full stop.[208]

SOLANIO. Ha!—what sayest thou?—Why, the end is, he hath lost a ship.

SALERIO. I would it might prove the end of his losses.

SOLANIO. Let me say *amen* betimes, lest the devil cross my prayer, for here he comes in the likeness of a Jew.—

[*Enter* SHYLOCK.]

How now, Shylock! what news among the merchants?

SHYLOCK. You know, none so well, none so well as you, of my daughter's flight.

SALERIO. That's certain: I, for my part, knew the tailor that made the wings she flew withal.[209]

---

[204] The Goodwin Sands, as they were called, lay off the eastern coast of Kent. The name was supposed to have been derived from Earl Godwin, whose lands were said to have been swallowed up there in the year 1100. In *King John*, v. 5, it is said that the supplies expected by the French "are cast away and sunk on Goodwin Sands."

[205] Here, as often, *of* is equivalent to *in respect of.*

[206] To *knap* is to *snap*, or to break into small pieces. So in 46th Psalm of *The Psalter*: "He *knappeth* the spear in sunder."

[207] The presumption being that by that time she has got so used to the thing as not to mind it much.

[208] That is, finish the sentence; or "say on till you come to a period."

[209] A sly allusion, probably, to the dress in which Jessica eloped.

SOLANIO. And Shylock, for his own part, knew the bird was fledged; and then it is the complexion[210] of them all to leave the dam.

SHYLOCK. She is damned for it.

SOLANIO. That's certain, if the devil may be her judge.

SHYLOCK. My own flesh and blood to rebel!

SOLANIO. Out upon it, old carrion! rebels it at these years?

SHYLOCK. I say, my daughter is my flesh and blood.

SALERIO. There is more difference between thy flesh and hers than between jet and ivory; more between your bloods than there is between red wine and Rhenish.[211] But tell us, do you hear whether Antonio have had any loss at sea or no?

SHYLOCK. There I have another bad match: a bankrupt, a prodigal, who dare scarce show his head on the Rialto; a beggar, that was used to come so smug[212] upon the mart; let him look to his bond: he was wont to call me usurer;—let him look to his bond: he was wont to lend money for a Christian courtesy;—let him look to his bond.

SALERIO. Why, I am sure, if he forfeit, thou wilt not take his flesh: what's that good for?

SHYLOCK. To bait fish withal: if it will feed nothing else, it will feed my revenge. He hath disgraced me, and hindered me half a million;[213] laughed at my losses, mocked at my gains, scorned my nation, thwarted my bargains, cooled my friends, heated mine enemies; and what's his reason? I am a Jew. Hath not a Jew eyes? hath not a Jew hands, organs, dimensions, senses, affections, passions? fed with the same food, hurt with the same weapons, subject to the same diseases, healed by the same means, warmed and cooled by the same winter and summer, as a Christian is? If you prick us, do we not bleed? if you tickle us, do we not laugh? if you poison us, do we not die? and if you wrong us, shall we not revenge? If we are like you in the rest, we will resemble you in that. If a Jew wrong a Christian, what is his humility? Revenge. If a Christian wrong a Jew, what should his sufferance be by Christian example? Why, revenge. The villainy you teach me, I will execute, and it shall go hard but I will better the instruction.[214]

---

[210] *Complexion* was much used for *nature, natural disposition,* or *temperament.* So, in the old tale upon which *Hamlet* was partly founded, the hero is spoken of as being a "Saturnist by *complexion.*"

[211] Rhenish wines are called white wines; named from the river Rhine.

[212] *Smug* is *brisk, gay,* or *spruce*; applied both to persons and things. Thus in *King Lear,* iv. 6: "I will die bravely, like a *smug* bridegroom: what, I will be jovial." And in *Henry IV., Part 1,* iii. 1: "Here the *smug* and silver Trent shall run in a new channel, fair and evenly."

[213] "Hinder'd me to the extent of half a million;" ducats, of course.

[214] "I will work mighty hard rather than fail to surpass my teachers."

[*Enter a* SERVANT.]

SERVANT. Gentlemen, my master Antonio is at his house and desires
to speak with you both.
SALERIO. We have been up and down to seek him.
SOLANIO. Here comes another of the tribe: a third cannot be matched,
unless the devil himself turn Jew.

[*Exeunt* SOLANIO, SALERIO, *and* SERVANT.]
[*Enter* TUBAL.]

SHYLOCK. How now, Tubal! what news from Genoa? hast thou found
my daughter?
TUBAL. I often came where I did hear of her, but cannot find her.
SHYLOCK. Why, there, there, there, there! a diamond gone, cost me
two thousand ducats in Frankfort! The curse never fell upon our
nation till now; I never felt it till now: two thousand ducats in that;
and other precious, precious jewels.—I would my daughter were
dead at my foot, and the jewels in her ear! would she were hearsed
at my foot, and the ducats in her coffin! No news of them?—Why,
so:—and I know not what's spent in the search: why, thou loss
upon loss! the thief gone with so much, and so much to find the
thief; and no satisfaction, no revenge: nor no in luck stirring but
what lights on my shoulders; no sighs but of my breathing; no tears
but of my shedding.
TUBAL. Yes, other men have ill luck too: Antonio, as I heard in
Genoa,—
SHYLOCK. What, what, what? ill luck, ill luck?
TUBAL.—hath an argosy cast away, coming from Tripolis.
SHYLOCK. I thank God, I thank God.—Is it true, is it true?
TUBAL. I spoke with some of the sailors that escaped the wreck.
SHYLOCK. I thank thee, good Tubal: good news, good news! ha,
ha!—where? in Genoa?
TUBAL. Your daughter spent in Genoa, as I heard, in one night
fourscore ducats.
SHYLOCK. Thou stickest a dagger in me: I shall never see my gold
again: fourscore ducats at a sitting! fourscore ducats!
TUBAL. There came divers of Antonio's creditors in my company to
Venice, that swear he cannot choose but break.
SHYLOCK. I am very glad of it: I'll plague him; I'll torture him: I am
glad of it.
TUBAL. One of them showed me a ring that he had of your daughter
for a monkey.

SHYLOCK. Out upon her! Thou torturest me, Tubal: it was my turquoise;[215] I had it of Leah when I was a bachelor: I would not have given it for a wilderness of monkeys.

TUBAL. But Antonio is certainly undone.

SHYLOCK. Nay, that's true, that's very true. Go, Tubal, fee me an officer;[216] bespeak him a fortnight before. I will have the heart of him, if he forfeit; for, were he out of Venice, I can make what merchandise I will. Go, go, Tubal, and meet me at our synagogue; go, good Tubal; at our synagogue, Tubal. [*Exeunt.*]

SCENE II.

Belmont. A Room in PORTIA'*s House.*

[*Enter* BASSANIO, PORTIA, GRATIANO, NERISSA, *and* ATTENDANTS.]

PORTIA. I pray you, tarry: pause a day or two
Before you hazard; for, in choosing wrong,
I lose your company: therefore forbear awhile.
There's something tells me,—but it is not love,—
I would not lose you; and you know yourself,
Hate counsels not in such a quality.
But lest you should not understand me well,—
And yet a maiden hath no tongue but thought,—
I would detain you here some month or two
Before you venture for me. I could teach you
How to choose right, but I am then forsworn;
So will I never be: so may you miss me;
But if you do, you'll make me wish a sin,
That I had been forsworn. Beshrew your eyes,
They have o'erlook'd[217] me and divided me;
One half of me is yours, the other half yours,—
Mine own, I would say; but if mine, then yours,
And so all yours. O, these naughty times
Put bars between the owners and their rights!
And so, though yours, not yours. Prove it so,[218]

---

[215] The turquoise was held precious not only for its rarity and beauty, but for the magical properties ascribed to it. Among other virtues, it was supposed to have the power of reconciling man and wife, and of forewarning the wearer, if any danger approached him. It was also thought to be a very compassionate stone; changing its colour, and looking pale and dim, if the wearer were ill.

[216] To *fee* an officer, or a lawyer, is to engage him by paying for his services in advance. Acceptance of such payment *binds* him.

[217] *O'erlook'd* is *eye-bitten;* that is, *bewitched* or *fascinated.*

Let fortune go to hell for it, not I.
I speak too long; but 'tis to piese[219] the time,
To eke it and to draw it out in length,
To stay you from election.
BASSANIO. Let me choose
For as I am, I live upon the rack.
PORTIA. Upon the rack, Bassanio! then confess
What treason there is mingled with your love.
BASSANIO. None but that ugly treason of mistrust,
Which makes me fear the enjoying of my love:[220]
There may as well be amity and life
'Tween snow and fire, as treason and my love.
PORTIA. Ay, but I fear you speak upon the rack,
Where men enforced do speak any thing.[221]
BASSANIO. Promise me life, and I'll confess the truth.
PORTIA. Well then, confess and live.
BASSANIO. *Confess* and *love*
Had been the very sum of my confession:
O happy torment, when my torturer
Doth teach me answers for deliverance![222]
But let me to my fortune and the caskets.

[*Curtain drawn from before the caskets.*]

PORTIA. Away, then! I am lock'd in one of them:
If you do love me, you will find me out.—
Nerissa and the rest, stand all aloof.—
Let music sound while he doth make his choice;
Then, if he lose, he makes a swan-like end,
Fading in music: that the comparison
May stand more proper, my eye shall be the stream

---

[218] That is, *if* it prove so, or *should* it prove so.—The meaning is, "if the event should prove that I, who am really yours in heart, am not to be yours in fact, or in hand, let the punishment fall upon fortune for misdirecting your choice, and not upon me."

[219] To *peise* is from *peser*, French; to *weigh* or *poise*. So in *Richard III.:* "Lest leaden slumber *peise* me down to-morrow." In the text it is used figuratively for to *suspend*, to *retard*; as *loadings*, thing in motion naturally makes it go slower.

[220] The Poet often has *doubt* for *fear* or *suspect*; here he has *fear* in the sense of *doubt*. "Fear the *not* of enjoying my love."

[221] It is pleasant to find Shakespeare before his age in denouncing the futility of this barbarous method of extorting truth. He was old enough to remember the case of Francis Throckmorton in 1584; and that of Squires in 1598 was fresh in his mind.—*Clarendon Editors.*

[222] Doubtless many a poor man whose office it was to work the rack, and whose heart had not been burnt to a cinder by theological rancour, had pity on the victim, and whispered in his ear "answers for deliverance"; prompting him to speak what might suffice for stopping the torture.

And watery death-bed for him.[223] He may win;
And what is music then? Then music is
Even as the flourish when true subjects bow
To a new-crowned monarch:[224] such it is
As are those dulcet sounds in break of day
That creep into the dreaming bridegroom's ear,
And summon him to marriage. Now he goes,
With no less presence,[225] but with much more love,
Than young Alcides, when he did redeem
The virgin tribute paid by howling Troy
To the sea-monster:[226] I stand for sacrifice
The rest aloof are the Dardanian wives,
With bleared visages, come forth to view
The issue of the exploit. Go, Hercules!
Live thou, I live: with much, much more dismay
I view the fight than thou that makest the fray.

[*Music, and the following* SONG, *whilst* BASSANIO *comments on the caskets to himself.*]

> *Tell me where is fancy bred,*[227]
> *Or in the heart, or in the head?*
> *How begot, how nourished?*

---

[223] Of course the allusion is to the habit, which the swan was imagined to have, of singing herself through the process of dying, or of going *out, fading,* in music. The closing part of the allusion supposes the bird to sing her life away while floating passively on the water.

[224] At English coronations, the act of putting on the crown was signalled by a joyous flourish of trumpets; whereupon the whole assembly were to bow their homage to the sovereign.

[225] *Presence* for *nobility of bearing* or *deportment.*

[226] The story, as told by Ovid, is, that Hesione, daughter of the Trojan King, being demanded by the Sea-monster, and being bound to a rock, Hercules slew the monster, and delivered her. Bassanio "goes with much more love," because Hercules went, not from love of the lady, but to gain the reward offered by Laomedon.

[227] This song is very artfully conceived, and carries something enigmatical or riddle-like in its face, as if on purpose to suggest or hint darkly the way to the right choice. The clew, however, is such as to be seized only by a man whose heart is thoroughly right in the matter he goes about. *Fancy,* as here used, means, apparently, that illusive power or action of the mind which has misled the other suitors, who, as Portia says, "have the wisdom by their wit to lose." And the illusion thus engendered in the eyes, and fed with gazing, dies just there where it is bred, as soon as it is brought to the test of experience by opening the wrong casket. The riddle evidently has some effect in starting Bassanio on the right track, by causing him to distrust such shows as catch the fancy or the eye,—the glitter of the gold and silver caskets.

Reply.

It is engender'd in the eyes,
With gazing fed; and fancy dies
In the cradle where it lies.
Let us all ring fancy's knell
I'll begin it,—Ding, dong, bell.

All.

Ding, dong, bell.

BASSANIO. So may the outward shows be least themselves:
    The world is still[228] deceived with ornament.
    In law, what plea so tainted and corrupt,
    But, being seasoned with a gracious voice,
    Obscures the show of evil? In religion,
    What damned error, but some sober brow
    Will bless it and approve[229] it with a text,
    Hiding the grossness with fair ornament?
    There is no vice so simple but assumes
    Some mark of virtue on his outward parts:
    How many cowards, whose hearts are all as false
    As stayers of sand,[230] wear yet upon their chins
    The beards of Hercules and frowning Mars;
    Who, inward search'd, have livers white as milk![231]
    And these assume but valour's excrement[232]
    To render them redoubted! Look on beauty,
    And you shall see 'tis purchased by the weight;[233]
    Which therein works a miracle in nature,
    Making them lightest that wear most of it:[234]

---

[228] *Still*, again, in its old sense of *always* or *continually*.

[229] *Approve* it is, simply, *prove* it, or *make* it *good*. This use of the word is very frequent in Shakespeare.

[230] *Stayers* in the sense of *props, supports*, or *stays*. The word is to be pronounced, here, as one syllable; as *cowards* also is.

[231] Cowards were commonly spoken of as having white livers. Shakespeare has *lily-livered* and *milk-livered* in the same sense; and Falstaff instructs us that "the second property of your excellent sherris is the warming of the blood; which, before cold and settled, left the liver white and pale, which is the badge of pusillanimity and cowardice."

[232] *Excrement*, from *excresco*, is used for every thing which appears to grow or vegetate upon the human body, as the hair, the beard, the nails.

[233] The meaning, here, is not very obvious; but the words are probably to be construed in the light of what follows. It would seem that false hair, "the golden tresses of the dead," was purchased at so much an ounce; and the more one had of it, the *vainer* one was.

So are those crisped snaky golden locks
Which make such wanton gambols with the wind,
Upon supposed fairness,[235] often known
To be the dowry of a second head,
The skull that bred them in the sepulchre.[236]
Thus ornament is but the guiled[237] shore
To a most dangerous sea; the beauteous scarf
Veiling an Indian feature;[238] in a word,
The seeming truth which cunning times put on
To entrap the wisest. Therefore, thou gaudy gold,
Hard food for Midas,[239] I will none of thee;
Nor none of thee, thou pale and common drudge
'Tween man and man: but thou, thou meagre lead,
Which rather threatenest than dost promise aught,
Thy paleness moves me more than eloquence;
And here choose I; joy be the consequence!
PORTIA. How all the other passions fleet to air,—
As doubtful thoughts, and rash-embraced despair,
And shuddering fear, and green-eyed jealousy! O love,
Be moderate; allay thy ecstasy,
In measure rein thy joy; scant this excess.
I feel too much thy blessing: make it less,
For fear I surfeit.
BASSANIO. [*Opening the leaden casket.*]What find I here?

---

[234] Another quibble upon *light*. See page 48, note 163. Here, however, it is between *light* as opposed to *heavy*, and *light* in the sense of *vanity*.

[235] That is, *imagined* or *imputed* fairness.—The Poet has often expressed a strong dislike of the custom, then in vogue, of wearing false hair. His 68th Sonnet has a passage very like that in the text:

> Thus in his cheek the map of days outworn,
> When beauty lived and died as flowers do now;
> Before the golden tresses of the dead,
> The right of sepulchres, were shorn away,
> To live a second life on second head;
> Ere beauty's dead fleece made another gay.

[236] "The skull *being* in the sepulchre." Ablative absolute.

[237] *Guiled*, if it be the right word, must here mean *seductive, beguiling*, or *full of guile*; the passive form with the active sense.

[238] *Feature* is used repeatedly by Shakespeare for *form, person*, or *personal appearance* in general. So in *The Two Gentlemen*, ii. 4: "He is complete in *feature* as in mind." Also in *King Lear*, iv. 2: "Thou changed and sex-cover'd thing, for shame, bemonster not thy *feature*!" And in *Cymbeline*, v. 5: "For *feature*, laming the shrine of Venus, or straight-pight Minerva, postures beyond brief nature;" where *shrine* is *statue* or image.

[239] Midas was a mythological personage who asked of God Bacchus that whatever he touched might be turned into gold. The request being granted, and all his food turning to gold in the eating, he implored Bacchus to revoke the favour.

Fair Portia's counterfeit![240] What demi-god
Hath come so near creation? Move these eyes?
Or whether, riding on the balls of mine,
Seem they in motion? Here are sever'd lips,
Parted with sugar breath: so sweet a bar
Should sunder such sweet friends. Here in her hairs
The painter plays the spider and hath woven
A golden mesh to entrap the hearts of men,
Faster than gnats in cobwebs; but her eyes,—
How could he see to do them? Having made one,
Methinks it should have power to steal both his
And leave itself unfurnish'd.[241] Yet look, how far
The substance of my praise doth wrong this shadow
In underprizing it, so far this shadow
Doth limp behind the substance. Here's the scroll,
The continent[242] and summary of my fortune.

                          [*Reads.*]

> *You that choose not by the view,*
> *Chance as fair and choose as true!*
> *Since this fortune falls to you,*
> *Be content and seek no new,*
> *If you be well pleased with this*
> *And hold your fortune for your bliss,*
> *Turn you where your lady is*
> *And claim her with a loving kiss.*

A gentle scroll.—Fair lady, by your leave; [*Kissing her.*]
I come by note, to give and to receive.[243]
Like one of two contending in a prize,
That thinks he hath done well in people's eyes,
Hearing applause and universal shout,

---

[240] *Counterfeit* was used for *likeness* or *portrait*. So in *The Wit of a Woman*, 1634: "I will see if I can agree with this stranger for the drawing of my daughter's *counterfeit*" And Hamlet calls the pictures he shows to his mother "the *counterfeit* presentment of two brothers."

[241] Unfurnished with a *companion*. In Fletcher's *Lover's Progress*, Alcidon says to Clarangé, on delivering Lidian's challenge, which Clarangé accepts,

> You are a noble gentleman.
> Will't please you bring a friend? we are two of us,
> And pity either, sir, should be *unfurnish'd*.

[242] *Continent*, in old English, is simply that which *contains* something.

[243] "I come in accordance with the written direction to give a kiss and to receive the lady."

Giddy in spirit, still gazing in a doubt
Whether these pearls of praise be his or no;
So, thrice fair lady, stand I, even so;
As doubtful whether what I see be true,
Until confirm'd, sign'd, ratified by you.
PORTIA. You see me, Lord Bassanio, where I stand,
Such as I am: though for myself alone
I would not be ambitious in my wish,
To wish myself much better; yet, for you
I would be trebled twenty times myself;
A thousand times more fair, ten thousand times more rich;
That only to stand high in your account,
I might in virtue, beauties, livings, friends,
Exceed account; but the full sum of me
Is sum of—something;[244] which, to term in gross,
Is an unlesson'd girl, unschool'd, unpractised;
Happy in this, she is not yet so old
But she may learn; happier than this,
She is not bred so dull but she can learn;
Happiest of all is that her gentle spirit
Commits itself to yours to be directed,
As from her lord, her governor, her king.
Myself and what is mine to you and yours
Is now converted: but now I was the lord[245]
Of this fair mansion, master of my servants,
Queen o'er myself: and even now, but now,
This house, these servants and this same myself
Are yours, my lord: I give them with this ring;
Which when you part from, lose, or give away,
Let it presage the ruin of your love
And be my vantage to exclaim on you.
BASSANIO. Madam, you have bereft me of all words,
Only my blood speaks to you in my veins;
And there is such confusion in my powers,
As after some oration fairly spoke
By a beloved prince, there doth appear
Among the buzzing pleased multitude;
Where every something, being blent together,
Turns to a wild of nothing, save of joy,
Express'd and not express'd. But when this ring
Parts from this finger, then parts life from hence:

---

[244] The dash before *something* is to indicate that the fair speaker hesitates for a term with which to describe herself modestly, yet without any affectation of modesty.

[245] The *lord* of a thing is, properly, the *owner* of it; hence the word is applicable to a woman as well as to a man.

O, then be bold to say Bassanio's dead!
NERISSA. My lord and lady, it is now our time,
    That have stood by and seen our wishes prosper,
    To cry, good joy: good joy, my lord and lady!
GRATIANO. My lord Bassanio and my gentle lady,
    I wish you all the joy that you can wish;
    For I am sure you can wish none from me:[246]
    And when your honours mean to solemnize
    The bargain of your faith, I do beseech you,
    Even at that time I may be married too.
BASSANIO. With all my heart, so thou canst get a wife.
GRATIANO. I thank your lordship, you have got me one.
    My eyes, my lord, can look as swift as yours:
    You saw the mistress, I beheld the maid;[247]
    You loved, I loved for intermission[248]
    No more pertains to me, my lord, than you.
    Your fortune stood upon the casket there,
    And so did mine too, as the matter falls;
    For wooing here until I sweat again,
    And sweating until my very roof was dry
    With oaths of love, at last,—if promise last,—
    I got a promise of this fair one here
    To have her love, provided that your fortune
    Achieved her mistress.
PORTIA. Is this true, Nerissa?
NERISSA. Madam, it is, so you stand pleased withal.
BASSANIO. And do you, Gratiano, mean good faith?
GRATIANO. Yes, faith, my lord.
BASSANIO. Our feast shall[249] be much honour'd in your marriage.
GRATIANO. We'll play with them the first boy for a thousand ducats.
NERISSA. What, and stake down?
GRATIANO. No; we shall ne'er win at that sport, and stake down.
    But who comes here? Lorenzo and his infidel?
    What, and my old Venetian friend Salerio?

---

    [246] "You have so much joy yourselves in each other, that you cannot grudge any to me."

    [247] We are not to understand by this that Nerissa is merely a servant-maid to Portia: she holds the place of companion or friend, and Portia all along treats her as such. They are as nearly equals in rank as Bassanio and Gratiano are, who are a pair of *friends*, not master and servant. Nor does it conflict with this, that Gratiano speaks of Portia as "her mistress"; for he is in a position that requires him to plead his present cause with a good deal of modesty and deference, lest he should seem to have abused his privilege of accompanying Bassanio on this loving voyage.

    [248] *Intermission* is *pause* or *delay*. Gratiano means, apparently, that he had been as prompt to fall in love as Bassanio.

    [249] *Shall* for *will*; the two being often used indiscriminately.

[*Enter* LORENZO, JESSICA, *and* SALERIO, *a* MESSENGER
from Venice.]

BASSANIO. Lorenzo and Salerio, welcome hither;
If that the youth of my new interest here
Have power to bid you welcome.—By your leave,
I bid my very[250] friends and countrymen,
Sweet Portia, welcome.
PORTIA. So do I, my lord:
They are entirely welcome.
LORENZO. I thank your honour.—For my part, my lord,
My purpose was not to have seen you here;
But meeting with Salerio by the way,
He did entreat me, past all saying nay,
To come with him along.
SALERIO. I did, my lord;
And I have reason for it. Signior Antonio
Commends him to you. [*Gives* BASSANIO *a letter.*]
BASSANIO. Ere I ope his letter,
I pray you, tell me how my good friend doth.
SALERIO. Not sick, my lord, unless it be in mind;
Nor well, unless in mind: his letter there
Will show you his estate. [BASSANIO *reads the letter.*]
GRATIANO. Nerissa, cheer yon stranger; bid her welcome.—
Your hand, Salerio: what's the news from Venice?
How doth that royal merchant, good Antonio?
I know he will be glad of our success;
We are the Jasons, we have won the fleece.
SALERIO. I would you had won the fleece that he hath lost.
PORTIA. There are some shrewd[251] contents in yon same paper,
That steals the colour from Bassanio's cheek:
Some dear friend dead; else nothing in the world
Could turn so much the constitution
Of any constant man. What, worse and worse!—
With leave, Bassanio: I am half yourself,
And I must freely have the half of anything
That this same paper brings you.
BASSANIO. O sweet Portia,
Here are a few of the unpleasant'st words
That ever blotted paper! Gentle lady,
When I did first impart my love to you,

---

[250] *Very*, here, is *real* or *true*; like the Latin *verus*.
[251] The proper meaning of *shrewd* is *sharp* or *biting*; hence *painful*.

I freely told you, all the wealth I had
Ran in my veins,—I was a gentleman;
And then I told you true: and yet, dear lady,
Rating myself at nothing, you shall see
How much I was a braggart. When I told you
My state[252] was nothing, I should then have told you
That I was worse than nothing; for, indeed,
I have engaged myself to a dear friend,
Engaged my friend to his mere[253] enemy,
To feed my means. Here is a letter, lady,—
The paper as the body of my friend,
And every word in it a gaping wound,
Issuing life-blood.—But is it true, Salerio?
Have all his ventures fail'd? What, not one hit?
From Tripolis, from Mexico and England,
From Lisbon, Barbary and India?
And not one vessel 'scape the dreadful touch
Of merchant-marring rocks?

SALERIO. Not one, my lord.
    Besides, it should[254] appear, that if he had
The present money to discharge the Jew,
He would not take it. Never did I know
A creature, that did bear the shape of man,
So keen and greedy to confound[255] a man:
He plies the duke at morning and at night,
And doth impeach the freedom of the state,
If they deny him justice: twenty merchants,
The duke himself, and the magnificoes
Of greatest port,[256] have all persuaded with him;
But none can drive him from the envious[257] plea
Of forfeiture, of justice and his bond.

JESSICA. When I was with him I have heard him swear
To Tubal and to Cush, his countrymen,
That he would rather have Antonio's flesh
Than twenty times the value of the sum
That he did owe him: and I know, my lord,

---

[252] *State* and *estate* were used interchangeably. So, a little before, we have *estate* for *state*, that is, *condition*: "Will show you his estate."

[253] Here, as often, *mere* is *absolute, entire*. So in *Othello*, ii. 2: "Certain tidings importing the *mere* perdition of the Turkish fleet."

[254] *Should*, again, where present usage requires *would*.

[255] To *ruin*, to *destroy*, is the more common meaning of to *confound*, in Shakespeare and the writers of his time.

[256] Of greatest *importance* or *consequence*. See page 23, note 27.

[257] *Envious* for *malicious*. So the word was constantly used. Also *envy* for *malice* or *hatred*.

If law, authority and power deny not,
It will go hard with poor Antonio.
PORTIA. Is it your dear friend that is thus in trouble?
BASSANIO. The dearest friend to me, the kindest man,
The best-condition'd and unwearied[258] spirit
In doing courtesies, and one in whom
The ancient Roman honour more appears
Than any that draws breath in Italy.
PORTIA. What sum owes he the Jew?
BASSANIO. For me three thousand ducats.
PORTIA. What, no more?
Pay him six thousand, and deface the bond;
Double six thousand, and then treble that,[259]
Before a friend of this description[260]
Shall lose a hair through Bassanio's fault.
First go with me to church and call me wife,
And then away to Venice to your friend;
For never shall you lie by Portia's side
With an unquiet soul. You shall have gold
To pay the petty debt twenty times over:
When it is paid, bring your true friend along.
My maid Nerissa and myself meantime
Will live as maids and widows. Come, away!
For you shall hence upon your wedding-day:
Bid your friends welcome, show a merry cheer:[261]
Since you are dear bought, I will love you dear.
But let me hear the letter of your friend.
BASSANIO. [*Reads.*] *Sweet Bassanio, my ships have all miscarried,*
my creditors grow cruel, my estate is very low, my bond to the Jew
is forfeit; and since in paying it, it is impossible I should live, all
debts are cleared between you and I, if I might but see you at my

---

[258] *Condition'd is tempered* or *disposed*. See page 29, note 66.—The force of the superlative, *best*, is continued over *unwearied*, in the sense of *most*. So in *The Witch* of Middleton, i. 2: "Call me the horrid'st and *unhallow'd* thing that life and nature tremble at." See, also, page 36, note 106.

[259] The Venetian ducat, in or near the Poet's time, is said to have been equivalent to nearly $1.53 of our money. At this rate, Portia's 36,000 ducats would have equalled about $55,000. And money was worth some six times as much then as it is now!—The coin took its name from the legend inscribed upon it: "Sit tibi, Christe, datus, quern tu regis, iste *ducatus*."

[260] Here, as often in this play, the ending *-tion* is properly dissyllabic, and was so pronounced in the Poet's time. The same with *complexion*, in ii. 1; and with *occasions*, in i. 1. Also with *-tian* in *Christian*, i. 3; and with *-cean* in *ocean*, i. 1. This is particularly the case when such a word ends a verse. Nevertheless it need not be pronounced so now, save when the rhyme requires it, as is very often the case in Spenser.

[261] *Cheer* is *look* or *countenance*; from the French *chere*. So in *A Midsummer-Night's Dream*, iii. 2: "All fancy-sick she is, and pale of *cheer*."

*death. Notwithstanding, use your pleasure: if your love do not
persuade you to come, let not my letter.*
PORTIA. O love, dispatch all business, and be gone!
BASSANIO. Since I have your good leave to go away,
　　I will make haste: but, till I come again,
　　No bed shall e'er be guilty of my stay,
　　No rest be interposer 'twixt us twain. [*Exeunt.*]

SCENE III.

Venice. A Street.

[*Enter* SHYLOCK, SALERIO, ANTONIO, *and* JAILER.]

SHYLOCK. Gaoler, look to him: tell not me of mercy.—
　　This is the fool that lent out money gratis.—
　　Gaoler, look to him.
ANTONIO. Hear me yet, good Shylock.
SHYLOCK. I'll have my bond; speak not against my bond:
　　I have sworn an oath that I will have my bond.
　　Thou call'dst me dog before thou hadst a cause;
　　But, since I am a dog, beware my fangs:
　　The duke shall grant me justice.—I do wonder,
　　Thou naughty gaoler, that thou art so fond[262]
　　To come abroad with him at his request.
ANTONIO. I pray thee, hear me speak.
SHYLOCK. I'll have my bond; I will not hear thee speak:
　　I'll have my bond; and therefore speak no more.
　　I'll not be made a soft and dull-eyed fool,
　　To shake the head, relent, and sigh, and yield
　　To Christian intercessors. Follow not;
　　I'll have no speaking: I will have my bond. [*Exit.*]
SALERIO. It is the most impenetrable cur
　　That ever kept[263] with men.
ANTONIO. Let him alone:
　　I'll follow him no more with bootless prayers.
　　He seeks my life; his reason well I know:
　　I oft deliver'd from his forfeitures
　　Many that have at times made moan to me;
　　Therefore he hates me.
SALERIO. I am sure the Duke
　　Will never grant this forfeiture to hold.

---

[262] *Fond*, again, in its old sense of *foolish.*
[263] *Kept*, here, is *dwelt* or *lived*; a common usage of the time.

ANTONIO. The Duke cannot deny the course of law:
For the commodity[264] that strangers have
With us in Venice, if it be denied,
Will much impeach the justice of his state;
Since that the trade and profit of the city
Consisteth of all nations.[265] Therefore, go:
These griefs and losses have so bated me,
That I shall hardly spare a pound of flesh
To-morrow to my bloody creditor.—
Well, gaoler, on.—Pray God, Bassanio come
To see me pay his debt, and then I care not! [*Exeunt.*]

SCENE IV.

Belmont. A Room in PORTIA'*s House.*

[*Enter* PORTIA, NERISSA, LORENZO, JESSICA, *and*
BALTHASAR.]

LORENZO. Madam, although I speak it in your presence,
You have a noble and a true conceit[266]
Of godlike amity; which appears most strongly
In bearing thus the absence of your lord.
But if you knew to whom you show this honour,
How true a gentleman you send relief,
How dear a lover[267] of my lord your husband,
I know you would be prouder of the work
Than customary bounty can enforce you.
PORTIA. I never did repent for doing good,
Nor shall not now: for in companions
That do converse and waste the time[268] together,
Whose souls do bear an equal yoke Of love,
There must be needs a like proportion[269]

---

[264] That is, *because of the commercial intercourse. For* is often thus equivalent to *because of.*

[265] Antonio was one of the citizens, while Shylock was reckoned among the strangers of the place. And, since the city was benefited as much by the trade and commerce of foreigners as of natives, justice evidently required that the law should give equal advantages to them both. But to stop the course of law in behalf of citizens against strangers, would be putting the latter at a disadvantage, and so would clearly impeach the justice of the State.

[266] *Conceit*, again, for *conception, idea,* or *judgment.* See page 22, note 21.

[267] *Lover* for *friend,* the two words being formerly synonymous.

[268] *Associate,* or *keep company,* and *spend* the time.

[269] *Proportion* sometimes has the sense of *form* or *shape.* So in *Richard III.*: "I that am curtail'd of this fair *proportion.*"

Of lineaments, of manners and of spirit;
Which makes me think that this Antonio,
Being the bosom lover of my lord,
Must needs be like my lord. If it be so,
How little is the cost I have bestow'd
In purchasing the semblance of my soul
From out the state of hellish misery!
This comes too near the praising of myself;
Therefore no more of it: hear other things.
Lorenzo, I commit into your hands
The husbandry[270] and manage of my house
Until my lord's return: for mine own part,
I have toward Heaven breathed a secret vow
To live in prayer and contemplation,
Only attended by Nerissa here,
Until her husband and my lord's return:
There is a monastery two miles off;
And there will we abide. I do desire you
Not to deny this imposition,[271]
The which my love and some necessity
Now lays upon you.
LORENZO. Madam, with all my heart;
I shall obey you in all fair commands.
PORTIA. My people do already know my mind,
And will acknowledge you and Jessica
In place of Lord Bassanio and myself.
And so farewell, till we shall meet again.
LORENZO. Fair thoughts and happy hours attend on you!
JESSICA. I wish your ladyship all heart's content.
PORTIA. I thank you for your wish, and am well pleased
To wish it back on you: fare you well Jessica.—

[*Exeunt* JESSICA *and* LORENZO.]

Now, Balthasar,
As I have ever found thee honest-true,
So let me find thee still. Take this same letter,
And use thou all the endeavour of a man
In speed to Padua: see thou render this
Into my cousin's hand, Doctor Bellario;

---

[270] The *ordering*. The literal meaning of *husband* is *house-band*, which is here
implied. Of course *manage* is *management*.

[271] *Imposition* is any charge, task, or duty *imposed* or *enjoined*.—Here, as also in
proportion and *contemplation*, the ending is properly dissyllabic. Also, in *companions*.
See page 71, note 260.

And, look, what notes and garments he doth give thee,
Bring them, I pray thee, with imagined speed[272]
Unto the Tranect,[273] to the common ferry
Which trades to Venice. Waste no time in words,
But get thee gone: I shall be there before thee.
BALTHASAR. Madam, I go with all convenient speed. [*Exit.*]
PORTIA. Come on, Nerissa; I have work in hand
That you yet know not of: we'll see our husbands
Before they think of us.
NERISSA. Shall they see us?
PORTIA. They shall, Nerissa; but in such a habit,
That they shall think we are accomplished
With that we lack. I'll hold thee any wager,
When we are both accoutred like young men,
I'll prove the prettier fellow of the two,
And wear my dagger with the braver grace,
And speak between the change of man and boy
With a reed voice, and turn two mincing steps
Into a manly stride, and speak of frays
Like a fine bragging youth, and tell quaint[274] lies,
How honourable ladies sought my love,
Which I denying, they fell sick and died;
I could not do withal:[275] then I'll repent,
And wish for all that, that I had not killed them;
And twenty of these puny lies I'll tell,
That men shall swear I have discontinued school
Above a twelvemonth. I have within my mind
A thousand raw tricks of these bragging Jacks,[276]
Which I will practise.
NERISSA. Why, shall we turn to men?
PORTIA. Fie, what a question's that,
If thou wert near a lewd interpreter!
But come, I'll tell thee all my whole device
When I am in my coach, which stays for us
At the park gate; and therefore haste away,

---

[272] With the celerity of imagination. So in the Chorus preceding the third Act of *Henry K*: "Thus with *imagined* wing our swift scene flies."

[273] This word evidently implies the name of a place where the passage-boat set out, and is in some way derived from *tranare*, to draw. No other instance of its use has yet occurred. The Poet had most likely heard or read of the place on the Brenta, about five miles from Venice, where a boat was *drawn* over a dam by a crane.

[274] *Quaint* is *ingenious, clever*, or *cunning*. See page 44, note 145.

[275] A phrase of the time, signifying *I could not help it*. So in Fletcher's *Little French Lawyer*: "*I cannot do withal*; I have spoke and spoke; I am betrayed and lost too." And in Chapman's *May-Day*, i. 1: "It is my infirmity, and *I cannot do withal*, to die for't."

[276] *Jack* was a common term of contempt.

For we must measure twenty miles to-day. [*Exeunt.*]

SCENE V.

The Same. A Garden.

[*Enter* LAUNCELOT *and* JESSICA.]

LAUNCELOT. Yes, truly; for, look you, the sins of the father are to be laid upon the children: therefore, I promise ye, I fear you.[277] I was always plain with you, and so now I speak my agitation[278] of the matter: therefore be of good cheer, for truly I think you are damned. There is but one hope in it that can do you any good; and that is but a kind of bastard hope neither.

JESSICA. And what hope is that, I pray thee?

LAUNCELOT. Marry, you may partly hope that your father got you not,—that you are not the Jew's daughter.

JESSICA. That were a kind of bastard hope, indeed: so the sins of my mother should be visited upon me.

LAUNCELOT. Truly then I fear you are damned both by father and mother: thus when I shun Scylla, your father, I fall into Charybdis,[279] your mother: well, you are gone both ways.

JESSICA. I shall be saved by my husband; he hath made me a Christian.

LAUNCELOT. Truly, the more to blame he: we were Christians enough before; e'en as many as could well live, one by another. This making Christians will raise the price of hogs: if we grow all to be pork-eaters, we shall not shortly have a rasher on the coals for money.

[*Enter* LORENZO.]

JESSICA. I'll tell my husband, Launcelot, what you say: here he comes.

LORENZO. I shall grow jealous of you shortly, Launcelot, if you thus get my wife into corners.

JESSICA. Nay, you need not fear us, Lorenzo: Launcelot and I are out. He tells me flatly, there is no mercy for me in Heaven, because I am a Jew's daughter: and he says, you are no good member of the

---

[277] Fear *for* you, or on your account. So in *Richard III.*, i. 1: "The king is sickly, weak, and melancholy, and his physicians *fear* him mightily."

[278] *Agitation* is a Gobboism for *cogitation.*

[279] This refers to a proverbial saying which has been traced back as far as to Saint Augustine: "Ne iterum quasi fugiens Charybdim, in Scyllam incurras." Halliwell quotes an old saying to the same purpose: "He got out of the muxy and fell into the pucksy."

commonwealth, for in converting Jews to Christians, you raise the price of pork.

LORENZO. I shall answer that better to the commonwealth than you can the getting up of the negro's belly: the Moor is with child by you, Launcelot.

LAUNCELOT. It is much that the Moor should be more than reason: but if she be less than an honest woman,[280] she is indeed more than I took her for.

LORENZO. How every fool can play upon the word! I think the best grace of wit will shortly turn into silence, and discourse grow commendable in none only but parrots.—Go in, sirrah; bid them prepare for dinner.

LAUNCELOT. That is done, sir; they have all stomachs.

LORENZO. Goodly Lord, what a wit-snapper are you! then bid them prepare dinner.

LAUNCELOT. That is done too, sir; only *cover* is the word.

LORENZO. Will you cover then, sir?

LAUNCELOT. Not so, sir, neither; I know my duty.[281]

LORENZO. Yet more quarrelling with occasion![282] Wilt thou show the whole wealth of thy wit in an instant? I pray tree, understand a plain man in his plain meaning: go to thy fellows; bid them cover the table, serve in the meat, and we will come in to dinner.

LAUNCELOT. For the table, sir, it shall be served in; for the meat, sir, it shall be covered; for your coming in to dinner, sir, why, let it be as humours and conceits shall govern. [*Exit.*]

LORENZO. O dear discretion, how his words are suited!
The fool hath planted in his memory
An army of good words; and I do know
A many fools, that stand in better place,
Garnish'd like him, that for a tricksy word
Defy the matter.[283]—How cheerest thou, Jessica?
And now, good sweet, say thy opinion,
How dost thou like the Lord Bassanio's wife?

JESSICA. Past all expressing. It is very meet

---

[280] What with the quibbles between *Moor* and *more*, and between *more* and *less*, Launcelot here approves himself a pretty swift punster.

[281] Launcelot is playing upon the two senses of *cover*, which was used both for setting the table and for putting on the hat.

[282] That is, going *at odds* or *in discord* with the occasion. Launcelot's punning is irrelevant to the matter in hand; *out of time*.

[283] To *defy* was often used for to *renounce, forsake*, or *give up*. So in *I Henry the Fourth*, i. 3: "All studies here I solemnly *defy*, save how to gall and pinch this Bolingbroke." Shakespeare alludes, no doubt, to the habit, which then infected all classes, of sacrificing their matter, or letting it go, in their fondness of verbal trickery and trifling, or in their chase after puns and plays upon words.—*Tricksy* is *artful, adroit*, or what we might call *smartish*.

The Lord Bassanio live an upright life;
For, having such a blessing in his lady,
He finds the joys of Heaven here on Earth;
And if on Earth he do not merit it,[284]
In reason he should never come to Heaven
Why, if two gods should play some Heavenly match
And on the wager lay two earthly women,
And Portia one, there must be something else
Pawn'd with the other, for the poor rude world
Hath not her fellow.
LORENZO. Even such a husband
Hast thou of me as she is for a wife.
JESSICA. Nay, but ask my opinion too of that.
LORENZO. I will anon: first, let us go to dinner.
JESSICA. Nay, let me praise you while I have a stomach.[285]
LORENZO. No, pray thee, let it serve for table-talk;
Then, howso'er thou speak'st, 'mong other things
I shall digest it.
JESSICA. Well, I'll set you forth. [*Exeunt.*]

ACT IV.

SCENE I.

Venice. A Court of Justice.

[*Enter the* DUKE, *the* MAGNIFICOES, ANTONIO, BASSANIO,
GRATIANO, SALERIO, *and others.*]

DUKE. What, is Antonio here?
ANTONIO. Ready, so please your grace.
DUKE. I am sorry for thee: thou art come to answer
A stony adversary, an inhuman wretch
uncapable of pity, void and empty
From any dram of mercy.
ANTONIO. I have heard
Your grace hath ta'en great pains to qualify[286]
His rigorous course; but since he stands obdurate
And that[287] no lawful means can carry me

---

[284] *It* refers to *blessing*, in the second line above.
[285] An equivoque on *stomach*, which is used in the two senses of inclination to praise and of appetite for food.
[286] To *abate*, to *assuage*, to *mitigate*, are old senses of *to qualify*.
[287] The old language in full was *since that*; and Shakespeare, in a second clause, often uses *that*, instead of repeating *since*. Here we should write "since—and *since*" It

Out of his envy's[288] reach, I do oppose
My patience to his fury, and am arm'd
To suffer, with a quietness of spirit,
The very tyranny and rage of his.
DUKE. Go one, and call the Jew into the court.
SALERIO. He is ready at the door: he comes, my lord.

[*Enter* SHYLOCK.]

DUKE. Make room, and let him stand before our face.—
Shylock, the world thinks, and I think so too,
That thou but lead'st this fashion of thy malice[289]
To the last hour of act; and then 'tis thought
Thou'lt show thy mercy and remorse,[290] more strange
Than is thy strange apparent cruelty;
And, where[291] thou now exact'st the penalty,—
Which is a pound of this poor merchant's flesh,—
Thou wilt not only loose[292] the forfeiture,
But, touch'd with human gentleness and love,
Forgive a moiety[293] of the principal;
Glancing an eye of pity on his losses,
That have of late so huddled on his back,
Enow to press a royal merchant[294] down
And pluck commiseration of his state
From brassy bosoms and rough hearts of flint,
From stubborn Turks and Tartars, never train'd
To offices of tender courtesy.
We all expect a gentle answer, Jew.
SHYLOCK. I have possess'd[295] your grace of what I purpose;
And by our holy Sabbath have I sworn
To have the due and forfeit of my bond:

---

was the same with *if, when, though,* and some others. *If that* has occurred several times in this play.

[288] *Envy* in its old sense of *malice* or *hatred.*

[289] "Keepest up this *manner* or *appearance* of malice."

[290] *Remorse,* in Shakespeare, generally means *pity* or *compassion.* The usage was common.

[291] *Where* for *whereas;* the two being used interchangeably.

[292] *Loose,* here, has the sense of *remit* or *release.*

[293] *Moiety* is, properly, *half,* but was used for any portion.

[294] "*Royal* merchant" is a complimentary phrase, to indicate the wealth and social standing of Antonio. In the Poet's time, Sir Thomas Gresham was so called, from his great wealth, and from his close financial relations with the Court and the Queen. The term was also applied to great Italian merchants, such as the Giustiniani and the Grimaldi, the Medici and the Pazzi, some of whom held mortgages on kingdoms and acquired the titles of princes for themselves.

[295] *Possess'd,* again, in its old sense of *informed.*

If you deny it, let the danger light
Upon your charter and your city's freedom.[296]
You'll ask me, why I rather choose to have
A weight of carrion flesh than to receive
Three thousand ducats: I'll not answer that:
But, say, it is my humour: is it answer'd?[297]
What if my house be troubled with a rat
And I be pleased to give ten thousand ducats
To have it baned? What, are you answer'd yet?
Some men there are love not a gaping pig;[298]
Some, that are mad if they behold a cat;
And others, when the bagpipe sings i' the nose,
Cannot contain their urine: for affection.[299]
Mistress of passion, sways it to the mood
Of what it likes or loathes.[300] Now, for your answer:
As there is no firm reason to be render'd,
Why he cannot abide a gaping pig;
Why he, a harmless necessary cat;
Why he, a woollen bag-pipe,[301] but of force[302]
Must yield to such inevitable shame
As to offend, himself being offended;
So can I give no reason, nor I will not,
More than a lodged hate and a certain loathing
I bear Antonio, that I follow thus
A losing suit against him. Are you answer'd?

---

[296] Perhaps the Poet had London in his mind, which held certain rights and franchises by royal charter, and was liable to have its charter revoked for an act of flagrant injustice.

[297] The meaning seems to be, "Suppose I should say," or, "What if I should say it is my humour; is that an answer?"—In the Poet's time, *humour* was used, much as *conscience* was at a later period, to justify any eccentric impulse of vanity, opinion, or self-will, for which no common ground of reason could be alleged. Thus, if a man had an individual crotchet which he meant should override the laws and conditions of our social being, it was his *humour*. Corporal Nym is a burlesque on this sort of affectation.

[298] A pig's head as roasted for the table. In England, a boar's head was served up at Christmas, with a lemon in its mouth. So in Webster's *Duchess of Malfi*, iii. 2: "He could not abide to see a pig's head gaping: I thought your Grace would find him a Jew." And in Fletcher's *Elder Brother*, ii. 2: "And they stand gaping like a roasted pig."

[299] Here, again, *for* is equivalent to *because of*. See page 73, note 264.—*Affection*, in this place, means much the same as *impulse*; more properly, the state of *being affected* or *moved* by any external object or impression.

[300] An axiomatic saying, brought in here with signal aptness. Even the greatest masters of passion move and rule it according as it is predisposed. Shakespeare's power lies partly in that fact: hence, in his work, the passions are rooted in the persons, instead of being merely pasted on.

[301] "*Wauling* bag-pipe" evidently means the same as "when the bag-pipe sings i' the nose." The effect in question is produced by the *sound* of the bag-pipe, and not by the *sight*, as in the other instances.

[302] *Of force* is the same as *perforce*; *of necessity*, or *necessarily*.

BASSANIO. This is no answer, thou unfeeling man,
  To excuse the current of thy cruelty.
SHYLOCK. I am not bound to please thee with my answers.
BASSANIO. Do all men kill the things they do not love?
SHYLOCK. Hates any man the thing he would not kill?
BASSANIO. Every offence is not a hate at first.
SHYLOCK. What, wouldst thou have a serpent sting thee twice?
ANTONIO. I pray you, think you question[303] with the Jew:
  You may as well go stand upon the beach
  And bid the main[304] flood bate his usual height;
  You may as well use question with the wolf
  Why he hath made the ewe bleat for the lamb;
  You may as well forbid the mountain pines
  To wag their high tops and to make no noise,
  When they are fretten with the gusts of Heaven;
  You may as well do anything most hard,
  As seek to soften that—than which what's harder?—
  His Jewish heart: therefore, I do beseech you,
  Make no more offers, use no farther means,
  But with all brief and plain conveniency
  Let me have judgment,[305] and the Jew his will.
BASSANIO. For thy three thousand ducats here is six.
SHYLOCK. What judgment shall I dread, doing
  Were in six parts and every part a ducat,
  I would not draw them; I would have my bond.
DUKE. How shalt thou hope for mercy, rendering none?
SHYLOCK. What judgment shall I dread, doing no wrong?
  You have among you many a purchased slave,
  Which, like your asses and your dogs and mules,
  You use in abject and in slavish parts,
  Because you bought them: shall I say to you,
  Let them be free, marry them to your heirs?
  Why sweat they under burthens? let their beds
  Be made as soft as yours and let their palates
  Be season'd with such viands? You will answer
  The slaves are ours. So do I answer you:
  The pound of flesh, which I demand of him,
  Is dearly bought; 'tis mine and I will have it.
  If you deny me, fie upon your law!
  There is no force in the decrees of Venice.

---

[303] *Question*, here, like *reason* before, has the sense of *talk* or *converse*. The usage was common, and Shakespeare has it repeatedly.

[304] *Great, strong, mighty* are among the old senses of *main*.

[305] "Let the sentence proceed against me with such promptness and directness as befits the administration of justice." The Poet often uses *brief* for *quick* or *speedy*.

I stand for judgment: answer; shall I have it?
DUKE. Upon my power I may dismiss this court,
Unless Bellario, a learned doctor,
Whom I have sent for to determine this,
Come here to-day.
SALERIO. My lord, here stays without
A messenger with letters from the doctor,
New come from Padua.
DUKE. Bring us the letter; call the messenger.
BASSANIO. Good cheer, Antonio! What, man, courage yet!
The Jew shall have my flesh, blood, bones and all,
Ere thou shalt lose for me one drop of blood.
ANTONIO. I am a tainted wether of the flock,
Meetest for death: the weakest kind of fruit
Drops earliest to the ground; and so let me
You cannot better be employ'd, Bassanio,
Than to live still and write mine epitaph.

[*Enter* NERISSA, *dressed like a Lawyer's Clerk.*]

DUKE. Came you from Padua, from Bellario?
NERISSA. From both, my lord. Bellario greets your grace.

[*Presenting a letter.*]

BASSANIO. Why dost thou whet thy knife so earnestly?
SHYLOCK. To cut the forfeiture from that bankrupt there.
GRATIANO. Not on thy sole, but on thy soul, harsh Jew,
Thou makest thy knife keen; but no metal can,
No, not the hangman's axe, bear half the keenness
Of thy sharp envy. Can no prayers pierce thee?
SHYLOCK. No, none that thou hast wit enough to make.
GRATIANO. O, be thou damn'd, inexorable dog!
And for thy life let justice be accused.[306]
Thou almost makest me waver in my faith
To hold opinion with Pythagoras,[307]
That souls of animals infuse themselves
Into the trunks of men: thy currish spirit

---

[306] "Let justice be impeached or arraigned for suffering thee to live."

[307] The ancient philosopher of Samos, who is said to have taught the transmigration of souls. In *As You Like It*, iii. 2, Rosalind says, "I was never so berhymed since Pythagoras' time, that I was an Irish rat, which I can hardly remember." And in *Twelfth Night*, iv. 2, the Clown says to Malvolio, "Thou shalt hold the opinion of Pythagoras ere I will allow of thy wits; and fear to kill a woodcock, lest thou dispossess the soul of thy grandam."

Govern'd a wolf, who, hang'd for human slaughter,
Even from the gallows did his fell soul fleet,
And, whilst thou lay'st in thy unhallow'd dam,
Infused itself in thee; for thy desires
Are wolvish, bloody, starved and ravenous.
SHYLOCK. Till thou canst rail the seal from off my bond,
Thou but offend'st thy lungs to speak[308] so loud:
Repair thy wit, good youth, or it will fall
To cureless ruin. I stand here for law.
DUKE. This letter from Bellario doth commend
A young and learned doctor to our court.—
Where is he?
NERISSA. He attendeth here hard by,
To know your answer, whether you'll admit him.
DUKE. With all my heart.—Some three or four of you
Go give him courteous conduct to this place.—
Meantime the court shall hear Bellario's letter.
CLERK. [*Reads.*] *Your grace shall understand that at the receipt of
your letter I am very sick: but in the instant that your messenger
came, in loving visitation was with me a young doctor of Rome; his
name is Balthasar. I acquainted him with the cause in controversy
between the Jew and Antonio the merchant: we turned o'er many
books together: he is furnished with my opinion; which, bettered
with his own learning, the greatness whereof I cannot enough
commend, comes with him, at my importunity, to fill up your
grace's request in my stead. I beseech you, let his lack of years be
no impediment to let him lack a reverend estimation;[309] for I never
knew so young a body with so old a head. I leave him to your
gracious acceptance, whose trial shall better publish his
commendation.*
DUKE. You hear the learn'd Bellario, what he writes:
And here, I take it, is the doctor come.

[*Enter* PORTIA, *dressed like a Doctor of Laws.*]

Give me your hand. Come you from old Bellario?
PORTIA. I did, my lord.
DUKE. You are welcome: take your place.
Are you acquainted with the difference
That holds this present question[310] in the court?
PORTIA. I am informed thoroughly[311] of the cause.

---

[308] That is, *in speaking*. The infinitive used gerundively again.

[309] "Let his youthfulness be no hindrance to his being reverently esteemed."

[310] "The *controversy* for the deciding of which the present *inquiry* or *investigation* is held." *Question* in its proper Latin sense.

Which is the merchant here, and which the Jew?
DUKE. Antonio and old Shylock, both stand forth.
PORTIA. Is your name Shylock?
SHYLOCK. Shylock is my name.
PORTIA. Of a strange nature is the suit you follow;
 Yet in such rule that the Venetian law
 Cannot impugn[312] you as you do proceed.
 [*To* ANTONIO.] You stand within his danger,[313] do you not?
ANTONIO. Ay, so he says.
PORTIA. Do you confess the bond?
ANTONIO. I do.
PORTIA. Then must the Jew be merciful.
SHYLOCK. On what compulsion must I? tell me that.
PORTIA. The quality of mercy is not strain'd;[314]
 It droppeth as the gentle rain from Heaven
 Upon the place beneath: it is twice blest;
 It blesseth him that gives and him that takes:
 'Tis mightiest in the mightiest:[315] it becomes
 The throned monarch better than his crown;
 His sceptre shows the force of temporal power,
 The attribute to awe and majesty,[316]
 Wherein doth sit the dread and fear of kings;
 But mercy is above this sceptred sway;
 It is enthroned in the hearts of kings,
 It is an attribute to God himself;
 And earthly power doth then show likest God's
 When mercy seasons justice. Therefore, Jew,
 Though justice be thy plea, consider this,—
 That, in the course of justice, none of us
 Should see salvation: we do pray for mercy;

---

[311] *Through* and *thorough* are but different forms of the same word.

[312] To *impugn* is to *controvert*, to *oppose*; literally, to *fight against*.

[313] "Within one's danger" properly meant within one's power or control, liable to a penalty which he might impose. Sometimes, however, it was used for being *in debt to one*. Here the meaning seems to be "Your life is in his power, and so in danger from him."

[314] That is, the nature of mercy is to act freely, not from constraint. Portia had used *must* in a moral sense, and the Jew purposely mistook it in a legal sense. This gives a natural occasion and impulse for her strain of "heavenly eloquence."

[315] This may mean, either that mercy exists in the greatest plenitude in Him who is omnipotent, or that the more power one has to inflict pain, the more he bows and subdues the heart by showing mercy. If the former, it should be printed "in the Mightiest." It was evidently a favourite idea with Shakespeare that the noblest and most amiable thing is power mixed with gentleness; and that the highest style of manhood is that which knows no fear of pain, but is a child to the touches of compassion.

[316] The *thing attributed* or *assigned* for the purpose of *inspiring* awe and of *symbolizing* majesty.

And that same prayer doth teach us all to render
The deeds of mercy.[317] I have spoke thus much
To mitigate the justice of thy plea;
Which if thou follow, this strict court of Venice
Must needs give sentence 'gainst the merchant there.
SHYLOCK. My deeds upon my head! I crave the law,
The penalty and forfeit of my bond.
PORTIA. Is he not able to discharge the money?
BASSANIO. Yes, here I tender it for him in the court;
Yea, twice the sum: if that will not suffice,
I will be bound to pay it ten times o'er,
On forfeit of my hands, my head, my heart:
If this will not suffice, it must appear
That malice bears down truth.[318] And I beseech you,
Wrest once the law to your authority:
To do a great right, do a little wrong,
And curb this cruel devil of his will.
PORTIA. It must not be; there is no power in Venice
Can alter a decree established:
'Twill be recorded for a precedent,
And many an error by the same example
Will rush into the state: it cannot be.
SHYLOCK. A Daniel come to judgment! yea, a Daniel!—
O wise young judge, how I do honour thee!
PORTIA. I pray you, let me look upon the bond.
SHYLOCK. Here 'tis, most reverend doctor, here it is.
PORTIA. Shylock, there's thrice thy money offer'd thee.
SHYLOCK. An oath, an oath, I have an oath in Heaven:
Shall I lay perjury upon my soul?
No, not for Venice.
PORTIA. Why, this bond is forfeit;[319]
And lawfully by this the Jew may claim
A pound of flesh, to be by him cut off
Nearest the merchant's heart.—Be merciful:
Take thrice thy money; bid me tear the bond.
SHYLOCK. When it is paid according to the tenor.

---

[317] "Portia, referring the Jew to the Christian doctrine of Salvation, and the Lord's Prayer, is a little out of character." So says Judge Blackstone; whereas the Lord's Prayer was itself but a compilation, all the petitions in it being taken out of the ancient euchologies or prayer-books of the Jews. So in Ecclesiasticus, xxviii. 2: "Forgive thy neighbour the hurt that he hath done unto thee, so shall thy sins also be forgiven when thou prayest."

[318] *Truth* is *honesty* here. A *true* man in old language is an *honest* man. And the honesty here shown is in offering to pay thrice the money.

[319] *Forfeit* for *forfeited*. This shortened preterite has occurred more than once before. See page 53, note 181.

It doth appear you are a worthy judge;
You know the law, your exposition
Hath been most sound: I charge you by the law,
Whereof you are a well-deserving pillar,
Proceed to judgment: by my soul I swear
There is no power in the tongue of man
To alter me: I stay here on my bond.
ANTONIO. Most heartily I do beseech the court
   To give the judgment.
PORTIA. Why then, thus it is:
   You must prepare your bosom for his knife;—
SHYLOCK. O noble judge! O excellent young man!
PORTIA.—For the intent and purpose of the law
   Hath full relation to the penalty,[320]
   Which here appeareth due upon the bond.
SHYLOCK. 'Tis very true: O wise and upright judge!
   How much more elder[321] art thou than thy looks!
PORTIA. Therefore lay bare your bosom.
SHYLOCK. Ay, his breast:
   So says the bond:—doth it not, noble judge?—
   Nearest his heart: those are the very words.
PORTIA. It is so. Are there balance here to weigh the flesh?
SHYLOCK. I have them ready.[322]
PORTIA. Have by some surgeon, Shylock, on your charge,
   To stop his wounds, lest he do bleed to death.
SHYLOCK. Is it so nominated in the bond?
PORTIA. It is not so express'd: but what of that?
   'Twere good you do so much for charity.
SHYLOCK. I cannot find it; 'tis not in the bond.
PORTIA. You, merchant, have you any thing to say?
ANTONIO. But little: I am arm'd and well prepared.—
   Give me your hand, Bassanio: fare you well!
   Grieve not that I am fallen to this for you;
   For herein Fortune shows herself more kind
   Than is her custom: it is still her use[323]
   To let the wretched man outlive his wealth,
   To view with hollow eye and wrinkled brow

---

[320] That is, the law relating to contracts is fully applicable in this case.

[321] Such double comparatives are frequent. So we have *more better*, *more braver*, and many others. Good grammar then.

[322] *Balance*, though singular in form, is used in a plural sense, referring to the *two scales* which make the balance. So in Baret's *Alvearie*, 1580: "Balances, or a payre of balance."

[323] It is *ever* her *custom* or *wont. Still* and *use* in these senses occur very often. The usage was common.

An age of poverty; from which lingering penance
Of such misery doth she cut me off.
Commend me to your honourable wife:
Tell her the process of Antonio's end;
Say how I loved you, speak me fair in death;[324]
And, when the tale is told, bid her be judge
Whether Bassanio had not once a love.
Repent but you that you shall lose your friend,
And he repents not that he pays your debt;
For if the Jew do cut but deep enough,
I'll pay it presently with all my heart.[325]

BASSANIO. Antonio, I am married to a wife
Which[326] is as dear to me as life itself;
But life itself, my wife, and all the world,
Are not with me esteem'd above thy life:
I would lose all, ay, sacrifice them all
Here to this devil, to deliver you.

PORTIA. Your wife would give you little thanks for that,
If she were by, to hear you make the offer.

GRATIANO. I have a wife, whom, I protest, I love:
I would she were in Heaven, so she could
Entreat some power to change this currish Jew.

NERISSA. 'Tis well you offer it behind her back;
The wish would make else an unquiet house.

SHYLOCK. [*Aside.*] These be the Christian husbands. I have a
daughter;
Would any of the stock of Barrabas[327]
Had been her husband rather than a Christian!—
[*Aloud.*] We trifle time: I pray thee, pursue sentence.

PORTIA. A pound of that same merchant's flesh is thine:
The court awards it, and the law doth give it.

SHYLOCK. Most rightful judge!

PORTIA. And you must cut this flesh from off his breast:
The law allows it, and the court awards it.

SHYLOCK. Most learned judge! A sentence!—Come, prepare!

PORTIA. Tarry a little; there is something else.
This bond doth give thee here no jot of blood;
The words expressly are *a pound of flesh*:
Take then thy bond, take thou thy pound of flesh;

---

[324] "Speak well of me when I am dead;" or, perhaps, "Tell the world that I died like a man."

[325] An equivoque on *heart*: and it rather heightens the pathos.

[326] *Which* and *who* were used indifferently, both of persons and things.

[327] Shakespeare seems to have followed the pronunciation usual in the theatre, *Barabbas* being sounded *Barabas* throughout Marlowe's *Jew of Malta*.

But, in the cutting it, if thou dost shed
One drop of Christian blood, thy lands and goods
Are, by the laws of Venice, confiscate
Unto the state of Venice.
GRATIANO. O upright judge!—Mark, Jew: O learned judge!
SHYLOCK. Is that the law?
PORTIA. Thyself shalt see the act:
For, as thou urgest justice, be assured
Thou shalt have justice, more than thou desirest.
GRATIANO. O learned judge!—Mark, Jew: a learned judge!
SHYLOCK. I take this offer, then;—pay the bond thrice
And let the Christian go.
BASSANIO. Here is the money.
PORTIA. Soft!
The Jew shall have all justice; soft! no haste:
He shall have nothing but the penalty.
GRATIANO. O Jew! an upright judge, a learned judge!
PORTIA. Therefore prepare thee to cut off the flesh.
Shed thou no blood, nor cut thou less nor more
But just a pound of flesh: if thou cut'st more
Or less than a just pound,—be't but so much
As makes it light or heavy in the substance,
Or the division of the twentieth part
Of one poor scruple, nay, if the scale do turn
But in the estimation of a hair,—
Thou diest and all thy goods are confiscate.
GRATIANO. A second Daniel, a Daniel, Jew!
Now, infidel, I have you on the hip.
PORTIA. Why doth the Jew pause? take thy forfeiture.
SHYLOCK. Give me my principal, and let me go.
BASSANIO. I have it ready for thee; here it is.
PORTIA. He hath refused it in the open court:
He shall have merely justice and his bond.
GRATIANO. A Daniel, still say I, a second Daniel!—
I thank thee, Jew, for teaching me that word.
SHYLOCK. Shall I not have barely my principal?
PORTIA. Thou shalt have nothing but the forfeiture,
To be so taken at thy peril, Jew.
SHYLOCK. Why, then the devil give him good of it!
I'll stay no longer question.
PORTIA. Tarry, Jew:
The law hath yet another hold on you.
It is enacted in the laws of Venice,
If it be proved against an alien
That by direct or indirect attempts

He seek the life of any citizen,
The party 'gainst the which he doth contrive
Shall seize one half his goods; the other half
Comes to the privy coffer of the state;
And the offender's life lies in the mercy
Of the duke only, 'gainst all other voice.
In which predicament, I say, thou stand'st;
For it appears, by manifest proceeding,
That indirectly and directly too
Thou hast contrived against the very life
Of the defendant; and thou hast incurr'd
The danger formerly by me rehearsed.
Down therefore and beg mercy of the duke.
GRATIANO. Beg that thou mayst have leave to hang thyself:
And yet, thy wealth being forfeit to the state,
Thou hast not left the value of a cord;
Therefore thou must be hang'd at the state's charge.
DUKE. That thou shalt see the difference of our spirits,
I pardon thee thy life before thou ask it:
For half thy wealth, it is Antonio's;
The other half comes to the general state,
Which humbleness may drive unto a fine.[328]
PORTIA. Ay, for the state, not for Antonio.[329]
SHYLOCK. Nay, take my life and all; pardon not that:
You take my house when you do take the prop
That doth sustain my house; you take my life
When you do take the means whereby I live.
PORTIA. What mercy can you render him, Antonio?
GRATIANO. A halter gratis; nothing else, for God's sake.
ANTONIO. So please my lord the duke and all the court
To quit the fine[330] for one half of his goods,
I am content; so he will let me have
The other half in use, to render it,
Upon his death, unto the gentleman
That lately stole his daughter:[331]

---

[328] "Submission on your part may move me to reduce it to a fine."

[329] Meaning, apparently, that the reduction of the forfeiture to a fine should apply only to that half of his goods which was to come to the coffer of the State, not that which fell to Antonio.

[330] If the court will *remit* the fine, or *acquit* Shylock of the forfeiture so far as the claim of the State is concerned. The Poet repeatedly uses *quit* thus for *acquit* or *release*.

[331] "That is, in trust for Shylock during his life, for the purpose of securing it at his death to Lorenzo. In conveyances of land, where it is intended to give the estate to any person after the death of another, it is necessary that a third person should be possessed of the estate, and the *use* be declared to the one after the death of the other, or the estate would be rendered insecure to the future possessor. This is called a conveyance to *uses*."

Two things provided more, that, for this favour,
He presently become a Christian;
The other, that he do record a gift,
Here in the court, of all he dies possess'd,
Unto his son Lorenzo and his daughter.
DUKE. He shall do this, or else I do recant
The pardon that I late pronounced here.
PORTIA. Art thou contented, Jew? what dost thou say?
SHYLOCK. I am content.
PORTIA. Clerk, draw a deed of gift.
SHYLOCK. I pray you, give me leave to go from hence;
I am not well: send the deed after me,
And I will sign it.
DUKE. Get thee gone, but do it.
GRATIANO. In christening shalt thou have two god-fathers:
Had I been judge, thou shouldst have had ten more,[332]
To bring thee to the gallows, not the font.

[*Exit* SHYLOCK.]

DUKE. Sir, I entreat you home with me to dinner.
PORTIA. I humbly do desire your Grace of pardon:[333]
I must away this night toward Padua,
And it is meet I presently set forth.
DUKE. I am sorry that your leisure serves you not.—
Antonio, gratify this gentleman,
For, in my mind, you are much bound to him.

[*Exeunt the* DUKE, MAGNIFICOES, *and his Train.*]

BASSANIO. Most worthy gentleman, I and my friend
Have by your wisdom been this day acquitted
Of grievous penalties; in lieu whereof,[334]
Three thousand ducats, due unto the Jew,
We freely cope[335] your courteous pains withal.

The anonymous author of the foregoing adds, that Shakespeare has rendered the old Latin law phrase pertaining to the case, "with all the strictness of a technical conveyancer, and has made Antonio desire to have one half of Shylock's goods in *use*,—to render it upon his death to Lorenzo."

[332] Meaning a jury of *twelve* men to condemn him. This appears to have been an old joke. So in *The Devil is an Ass*, by Ben Jonson: "I will leave you to your godfathers in law. Let *twelve men* work."

[333] An old English idiom now obsolete. So in *A Midsummer-Night's Dream*, iii. 1: "I shall desire you of more acquaintance."

[334] In *return for* which, or *in consideration of* which. So the phrase is, I think, always used in Shakespeare.

ANTONIO. And stand indebted, over and above,
In love and service to you evermore.
PORTIA. He is well paid that is well satisfied;
And I, delivering you, am satisfied
And therein do account myself well paid:
My mind was never yet more mercenary.
I pray you, know me when we meet again:
I wish you well, and so I take my leave.
BASSANIO. Dear sir, of force I must attempt you further:
Take some remembrance of us, as a tribute,
Not as a fee: grant me two things, I pray you,—
Not to deny me, and to pardon me.
PORTIA. You press me far, and therefore I will yield.—
[*To* ANTONIO.] Give me your gloves, I'll wear them for your
sake;—
[*To* BASSANIO.] And, for your love, I'll take this ring from you:
Do not draw back your hand; I'll take no more;
And you in love shall[336] not deny me this.
BASSANIO. This ring, good sir,—alas, it is a trifle!
I will not shame myself to give you this.
PORTIA. I will have nothing else but only this;
And now methinks I have a mind to it.
BASSANIO. There's more depends on this than on the value.
The dearest ring in Venice will I give you,
And find it out by proclamation:
Only for this, I pray you, pardon me.
PORTIA. I see, sir, you are liberal in offers
You taught me first to beg; and now methinks
You teach me how a beggar should be answer'd.
BASSANIO. Good sir, this ring was given me by my wife;
And when she put it on, she made me vow
That I should neither sell nor give nor lose it.
PORTIA. That 'scuse serves many men to save their gifts.
An if[337] your wife be not a mad-woman,
And know how well I have deserved the ring,
She would not hold out enemy for ever,
For giving it to me. Well, peace be with you!

---

[335] The only instance I have met with of *cope* being used in the sense of *requite*. A like use of the word in composition, however, occurs in Ben Jonson's *Fox*, iii. 5:

> He would have sold his part of Paradise
> For ready money, had he met a *cope-man.*

[336] *Shall*, again, where we should use will. See page 68, note 249.
[337] *An if* is an old reduplication, with the sense merely of *if.* So the old writers use *an*, or *if*, or *an if*, indifferently.

[*Exeunt* PORTIA *and* NERISSA.]

ANTONIO. My Lord Bassanio, let him have the ring:
    Let his deservings and my love withal
    Be valued against your wife's commandment.[338]
BASSANIO. Go, Gratiano, run and overtake him;
    Give him the ring, and bring him, if thou canst,
    Unto Antonio's house: away! make haste.—

[*Exit* GRATIANO.]

Come, you and I will thither presently;
    And in the morning early will we both
    Fly toward Belmont: come, Antonio. [*Exeunt.*]

SCENE II.

The Same. A Street.

[*Enter* PORTIA *and* NERISSA, *disguised as before.*]

PORTIA. Inquire the Jew's house out, give him this deed
    And let him sign it: we'll away to-night
    And be a day before our husbands home:
    This deed will be well welcome to Lorenzo.

[*Enter* GRATIANO.]

GRATIANO. Fair sir, you are well o'erta'en
    My Lord Bassanio upon more advice,[339]
    Hath sent you here this ring, and doth entreat
    Your company at dinner.
PORTIA. That cannot be:
    His ring I do accept most thankfully;
    And so, I pray you, tell him: furthermore,
    I pray you, show my youth old Shylock's house.
GRATIANO. That will I do.
NERISSA. Sir, I would speak with you.—
    [*To* PORTIA.] I'll see if I can get my husband's ring,

---

[338] *Commandment* is properly four syllables here, as if written *commandement*. And so, in fact, it is spelt in the old copies. Perhaps the old spelling should in such cases be retained.

[339] Upon *further consideration.* See page 24, note 31. And so in *Henry the Fifth,* ii. 2: "It was excess of wine that set him on; and, on our *more advice,* we pardon him."

Which I did make him swear to keep for ever.
PORTIA. Thou mayst, I warrant. We shall have old[340] swearing
That they did give the rings away to men;
But we'll outface them, and outswear them too.
Away! make haste: thou know'st where I will tarry.
NERISSA. Come, good sir, will you show me to this house?

[*Exeunt.*]

ACT V.

SCENE I.

Belmont. Pleasure-grounds of PORTIA's *House.*

[*Enter* LORENZO *and* JESSICA.]

LORENZO. The moon shines bright: in such a night as this,
When the sweet wind did gently kiss the trees
And they did make no noise,—in such a night
Troilus methinks mounted the Trojan walls
And sigh'd his soul toward the Grecian tents,
Where Cressid lay that night.[341]
JESSICA. In such a night
Did Thisbe fearfully o'ertrip the dew
And saw the lion's shadow ere himself,[342]
And ran dismay'd away.
LORENZO. In such a night
Stood Dido with a willow[343] in her hand
Upon the wild sea banks and waft her love
To come again to Carthage.
JESSICA. In such a night
Medea gather'd the enchanted herbs
That did renew old Æson.[344]

---

[340] *Old* was a frequent intensive in colloquial speech; very much as *huge* is used now. So in *Much Ado*, v. 2: "Yonder's *old* coil at home." And in *The Merry Wives*, i. 4: "Here will be an *old* abusing of God's patience and the king's English."

[341] The story of Troilus and Cressida is dramatized in Shakespeare's play of that name. Troilus was a Trojan prince, one of King Priam's fifty sons. He fell deeply and most honourably in love with Cressida, who, after being mighty sweet upon him, forsook him for his enemy, Diomedes the Greek; which he took to heart prodigiously.

[342] That is, ere she saw the lion himself. The story of "Pyramus and his love Thisbe" is burlesqued in the interlude of Bottom and company in *A Midsummer-Night's Dream.*

[343] Spenser in like sort makes the willow a symbol of forsaken love. So in *The Faerie Queene*, i . 1, 9: "The willow, worne of forlorne paramours."

LORENZO. In such a night
Did Jessica steal from the wealthy Jew
And with an unthrift love did run from Venice
As far as Belmont.
JESSICA. In such a night
Did young Lorenzo swear he loved her well,
Stealing her soul with many vows of faith
And ne'er a true one.
LORENZO. In such a night
Did pretty Jessica, like a little shrew,
Slander her love, and he forgave it her.
JESSICA. I would out-night you, did no body come;
But, hark, I hear the footing of a man.

[*Enter* STEPHANO.]

LORENZO. Who comes so fast in silence of the night?
STEPHANO. A friend.
LORENZO. A friend! what friend? your name, I pray you, friend?
STEPHANO. Stephano is my name;[345] and I bring word
My mistress will before the break of day
Be here at Belmont; she doth stray about
By holy crosses, where she kneels and prays
For happy wedlock hours.[346]
LORENZO. Who comes with her?
STEPHANO. None but a holy hermit and her maid.
I pray you, is my master yet return'd?
LORENZO. He is not, nor we have not heard from him.—
But go we in, I pray thee, Jessica,
And ceremoniously let us prepare
Some welcome for the mistress of the house.

---

[344] Twice before in this play we have had allusions to the story of Jason and his voyage to Colchos in quest of the golden fleece. Medea, daughter to the King of Colchos, fell in love with him, helped him to win the fleece, then stole her father's treasure, and ran away with Jason to Greece. Now Jason's father was very old and decayed; and Medea was a potent enchantress, the most so of all the ancient girls: so, with "the hidden power of herbs and might of magic spell," she made a most plenipotent broth, wherewith she renewed the old man's youth. Ovid has it, that she did this by drawing the blood out of his veins, and filling them with the broth.

[345] In this play the name *Stephano* has the accent on the second syllable. In *The Tempest*, written some years later, the same name has it, rightly, on the first.

[346] In old times crosses were set up at the intersection of roads, and in other places specially associated with saintly or heroic names, to invite the passers-by to devotion. And in those days Christians were much in the habit of remembering in their prayers whatever lay nearest their hearts. The Poet has the same old thought still more sweetly in two other places.

[*Enter* LAUNCELOT.]

LAUNCELOT. Sola, sola! wo ha, ho! sola, sola!
LORENZO. Who calls?
LAUNCELOT. Sola!—did you see Master Lorenzo and Mistress
Lorenzo?—sola, sola!
LORENZO. Leave hollaing, man: here.
LAUNCELOT. Sola!—where? where?
LORENZO. Here.
LAUNCELOT. Tell him there's a post come from my master, with his
    horn full of good news:[347] my master will be here ere morning.
    [*Exit.*]
LORENZO. Sweet soul, let's in, and there expect their coming.
    And yet no matter: why should we go in?
    My friend Stephano, signify, I pray you,
    Within the house, your mistress is at hand;
    And bring your music forth into the air.—[*Exit* STEPHANO.]
    How sweet the moonlight sleeps upon this bank!
    Here will we sit and let the sounds of music
    Creep in our ears: soft stillness and the night
    Become the touches of sweet harmony.
    Sit, Jessica. Look how the floor of Heaven
    Is thick inlaid with patines[348] of bright gold:
    There's not the smallest orb which thou behold'st
    But in his motion like an angel sings,
    Still quiring[349] to the young-eyed cherubins;
    Such harmony is in immortal souls;[350]

---

[347] The postman used to carry a horn, and blow it to give notice of his coming, on approaching a place where he had something to deliver. Launcelot has just been imitating the notes of the horn in his exclamations, *Sola,* &c.—*Expect,* in the next line, is *wait for* or *await.* The Poet has it repeatedly in that sense. And so in Hebrews, x. 13: "From henceforth *expecting* till his enemies be made his footstool."

[348] A small plate, used in the administration of the Eucharist: it was commonly of gold, or silver-gilt.

[349] Continually sounding an accompaniment.—Of course everybody has heard of "the music of the spheres,"—an ancient mystery which taught that the heavenly bodies in their revolutions sing together in a concert so loud, various, and sweet, as to exceed all proportion to the human ear. And the greatest souls, from Plato to Wordsworth, have been lifted above themselves, with the idea that the universe was knit together by a principle of which musical harmony is the aptest and clearest expression. Milton touches it with surpassing sweetness in the morning hymn of Adam and Eve, *Paradise Lost,* v. 177: "And ye five other wandering fires, that move in mystic dance not without song, resound His praise," &c. See, also, Milton's *Arcades,* and Coleridge's *Remorse,* Act iii., scene 1, and Wordsworth's great poem *On the Power of Sound,* stanza xii.

[350] So in Hooker's *Ecclesiastical Polity,* v. 38: "Touching musical harmony, such is the force thereof, and so pleasing effects it hath in that very part of man which is most divine, that some have thereby been induced to think that *the soul itself by nature is or hath in it harmony.*

But whilst this muddy vesture of decay
Doth grossly close it in, we cannot hear it.—

[*Enter Musicians.*]

Come, ho! and wake Diana with a hymn!
With sweetest touches pierce your mistress' ear,
And draw her home with music. [*Music.*]
JESSICA. I am never merry when I hear sweet music.
LORENZO. The reason is, your spirits are attentive:
For do but note a wild and wanton herd,
Or race of youthful and unhandled colts,
Fetching mad bounds, bellowing and neighing loud,
Which is the hot condition of their blood;
If they but hear perchance a trumpet sound,
Or any air of music touch their ears,
You shall perceive them make a mutual stand,
Their savage eyes turn'd to a modest gaze
By the sweet power of music: therefore the poet
Did feign that Orpheus drew trees, stones and floods;
Since nought so stockish, hard and full of rage,
But music for the time doth change his nature.
The man that hath no music in himself,
Nor is not moved with concord of sweet sounds,
Is fit for treasons, stratagems and spoils;
The motions of his spirit are dull as night
And his affections dark as Erebus:[351]
Let no such man be trusted.[352] Mark the music.

[*Enter* PORTIA *and* NERISSA.]

---

[351] *Erebus* was the darkest and gloomiest region of Hades.

[352] Upon the general subject of this splendid strain touching music and musical harmony, it seems but just to quote a passage hardly inferior from Sir Thomas Browne, *Religio Medici*; Part ii., Sect. 9: "There is a music wherever there is harmony, order, or proportion ; and thus far we may maintain 'the music of the spheres': for those well-ordered motions and regular paces, though they give no sound unto the ear, yet to the understanding they strike a note most full of harmony. Whatsoever is harmonically composed delights in harmony; which makes me much distrust the symmetry of those heads which declaim against all church-music. For myself, not only from my obedience but my particular genius I do embrace it: for even that vulgar and tavern music which makes one man merry, another mad, strikes in me a deep fit of devotion, and a profound contemplation of the first Composer. There is something in it of divinity more than the ear discovers: it is an hieroglyphical and shadowed lesson of the whole world and creatures of God,—such a melody to the ear as the whole world, well understood, would afford the understanding. In brief, it is a sensible fit of that harmony which intellectually sounds in the ear of God. I will not say, with Plato, the soul is an harmony, but harmonical, and hath its nearest sympathy unto music."

PORTIA. That light we see is burning in my hall.
How far that little candle throws his beams!
So shines a good deed in a naughty world.
NERISSA. When the moon shone, we did not see the candle.
PORTIA. So doth the greater glory dim the less:
A substitute shines brightly as a king
Unto the king be by, and then his state
Empties itself, as doth an inland brook
Into the main of waters. Music! hark!
NERISSA. It is your music, madam, of the house.
PORTIA. Nothing is good, I see, without respect:[353]
Methinks it sounds much sweeter than by day.
NERISSA. Silence bestows that virtue on it, madam.
PORTIA. The crow doth sing as sweetly as the lark,
When neither is attended, and I think
The nightingale, if she should sing by day,
When every goose is cackling, would be thought
No better a musician than the wren.[354]
How many things by season season'd[355] are
To their right praise and true perfection!—
Peace, ho! the moon sleeps with Endymion,[356]
And would not be awaked. [*Music ceases.*]
LORENZO. That is the voice,
Or I am much deceived, of Portia.
PORTIA. He knows me as the blind man knows the cuckoo,
By the bad voice.
LORENZO. Dear lady, welcome home.
PORTIA. We have been praying for our husbands' healths,
Which speed, we hope, the better for our words.
Are they return'd?
LORENZO. Madam, they are not yet;
But there is come a messenger before,

---

[353] Nothing is good unless it be *regarded, heeded,* or *attended to.* Hence the music sounds much better when there is nothing to distract or divert the attention. This explanation is justified by what Portia says in the second speech after.

[354] "The difference is in the hearer's mind, and not in the songs themselves; and the nightingale is reputed the first of songsters because she sings at the time when she can best be heard." We have a like thought in the Poet's 102d Sonnet.

[355] A rather unpleasant jingle in *season* and *season'd.* The meaning is, that, by being rightly *timed,* the things are tempered and made fit for their purpose; hence *relished.*

[356] Endymion was a very beautiful youth: Juno took a fancy to him, whereupon Jupiter grew jealous of him, and cast him into a perpetual sleep on Mount Latmos. While he was there asleep, Luna got so smitten with his beauty, that she used to come down and kiss him, and lie by his side. Some said, however, that Luna herself put him asleep, that she might have the pleasure of kissing him without his knowing it, the youth being somewhat shy when awake. The story was naturally a favorite with the poets.

To signify their coming.

PORTIA. Go in, Nerissa;

Give order to my servants that they take

No note at all of our being absent hence;—

Nor you, Lorenzo;—Jessica, nor you. [*A tucket*[357] *sounds.*]

LORENZO. Your husband is at hand; I hear his trumpet:

We are no tell-tales, madam; fear you not.

PORTIA. This night methinks is but the daylight sick;

It looks a little paler: 'tis a day,

Such as the day is when the sun is hid.

[*Enter* BASSANIO, ANTONIO, GRATIANO, *and their Followers.*]

BASSANIO. We should hold day with the Antipodes,[358]

If you would walk in absence of the sun.

PORTIA. Let me give light, but let me not be light;[359]

For a light wife doth make a heavy husband,

And never be Bassanio so for me:

But God sort all![360] You are welcome home, my lord.

BASSANIO. I thank you, madam. Give welcome to my friend.

This is the man, this is Antonio,

To whom I am so infinitely bound.

PORTIA. You should in all sense'[361] be much bound to him.

For, as I hear, he was much bound for you.

ANTONIO. No more than I am well acquitted of.

PORTIA. Sir, you are very welcome to our house:

It must appear in other ways than words,

Therefore I scant this breathing courtesy.[362]

GRATIANO. [*To* NERISSA.] By yonder moon I swear you do me wrong;

In faith, I gave it to the judge's clerk:

Would he were gelt that had it, for my part,

Since you do take it, love, so much at heart.

PORTIA. A quarrel, ho, already! what's the matter?

GRATIANO. About a hoop of gold, a paltry ring

---

[357] A *tucket* is a peculiar series of notes on a trumpet. Probably the word is from the Italian *toccata*, which is said to mean a prelude to a sonata.

[358] This is making Portia pretty luminous or radiant. To "hold day with the Antipodes" is to have day at the same time with them.

[359] Twice before in these scenes, we have had playing upon *light*: here it is especially graceful and happy. See page 65, note 234.

[360] *Sort* here has the sense of the Latin *sortior*: "God *allot* all," or *dispose* all.

[361] Is *sense'* used for *reason* here? Perhaps *all sense* is put for *every sense* or *all senses*. So the Poet has *house'* for *houses*, *horse'* for *horses*, &c.

[362] This complimentary form, made up only of *breath*.

That she did give me, whose posy was
For all the world like cutler's poetry
Upon a knife,[363] *Love me, and leave me not.*
NERISSA. What talk you of the posy or the value?
You swore to me, when I did give it you,
That you would wear it till your hour of death
And that it should lie with you in your grave:
Though not for me, yet for your vehement oaths,
You should have been respective,[364] and have kept it.
Gave it a judge's clerk! no, God's my judge,
The clerk will ne'er wear hair on's face that had it.
GRATIANO. He will, an if he live to be a man.
NERISSA. Ay, if a woman live to be a man.
GRATIANO. Now, by this hand, I gave it to a youth,
A kind of boy, a little scrubbed[365] boy,
No higher than thyself; the judge's clerk,
A prating boy, that begg'd it as a fee:
I could not for my heart deny it him.
PORTIA. You were to blame,—I must be plain with you,—
To part so slightly with your wife's first gift;
A thing stuck on with oaths upon your finger
And so riveted with faith unto your flesh.
I gave my love a ring and made him swear
Never to part with it; and here he stands;
I dare be sworn for him he would not leave it
Nor pluck it from his finger, for the wealth
That the world masters. Now, in faith, Gratiano,
You give your wife too unkind a cause of grief:
An 'twere to me, I should be mad at it.
BASSANIO. [*Aside.*] Why, I were best to cut my left hand off
And swear I lost the ring defending it.
GRATIANO. My Lord Bassanio gave his ring away
Unto the judge that begg'd it and indeed
Deserved it too; and then the boy, his clerk,
That took some pains in writing, he begg'd mine;
And neither man nor master would take aught
But the two rings.

---

[363] Knives were formerly inscribed, by means of *aqua* fortis, with short sentences in distich. The *posy* of a ring was the motto.

[364] *Respective* is *considerate* or *regardful*; in the same sense as *respect* is explained, page 21, note 19. The word is repeatedly used thus by Shakespeare; as in *Romeo and Juliet*, iii. 1: "Away to Heaven *respective* lenity, and fire-eyed fury be my conduct now!"

[365] *Scrubbed* is here used in the sense of *stunted*; as in Holland's Pliny: "Such will never prove fair trees, but *scrubs* only." And Verplanck observes that the name *scrub oak* was from the first settlement of this country given to the dwarf or bush oak.

PORTIA. What ring gave you my lord?
    Not that, I hope, which you received of me.
BASSANIO. If I could add a lie unto a fault,
    I would deny it; but you see my finger
    Hath not the ring upon it,—it is gone.
PORTIA. Even so void is your false heart of truth.
    By Heaven, I will ne'er come in your bed
    Until I see the ring.
NERISSA. Nor I in yours
    Till I again see mine.
BASSANIO. Sweet Portia,
    If you did know to whom I gave the ring,
    If you did know for whom I gave the ring
    And would conceive for what I gave the ring
    And how unwillingly I left the ring,
    When nought would be accepted but the ring,
    You would abate the strength of your displeasure.
PORTIA. If you had known the virtue of the ring,
    Or half her worthiness that gave the ring,
    Or your own honour to contain[366] the ring,
    You would not then have parted with the ring.
    What man is there so much unreasonable,
    If you had pleased to have defended it
    With any terms of zeal, wanted the modesty
    To urge the thing held as a ceremony?
    Nerissa teaches me what to believe:
    I'll die for't but some woman had the ring.
BASSANIO. No, by my honour, madam, by my soul,
    No woman had it, but a Civil Doctor,[367]
    Which did refuse three thousand ducats of me
    And begg'd the ring; the which I did deny him
    And suffer'd him to go displeased away;
    Even he that did uphold the very life
    Of my dear friend. What should I say, sweet lady?
    I was enforced to send it after him;
    I was beset with shame and courtesy;[368]
    My honour would not let ingratitude

---

[366] *Contain* was sometimes used in the sense of *retain*. So in Bacon's *Essays*: "To *containe* anger from mischiefe, though it take hold of a man, there be two things."

[367] A *Civil Doctor* is a doctor of the Civil Law.

[368] "Shame and courtesy" is here put for *shame of discourtesy*. The Poet has several like expressions. In *King Lear*, i. 2: "This policy and reverence of age"; which means "This policy, or custom, *of reverencing* age." Also in i. 5: "This milky *gentleness and course* of yours;" that is, milky *and gentle* course. And *Hamlet*, i. 1: "Well ratified by law *and* heraldry;" meaning the law *of* heraldry.

So much besmear it. Pardon me, good lady;
For, by these blessed candles of the night,[369]
Had you been there, I think you would have begg'd
The ring of me to give the worthy doctor.

PORTIA. Let not that doctor e'er come near my house:
Since he hath got the jewel that I loved,
And that which you did swear to keep for me,
I will become as liberal as you;
I'll not deny him any thing I have,
No, not my body nor my husband's bed:
Know him I shall, I am well sure of it:
Lie not a night from home; watch me like Argus:
If you do not, if I be left alone,
Now, by mine honour, which is yet mine own,
I'll have that doctor for my bedfellow.

NERISSA. And I his clerk; therefore be well advised[370]
How you do leave me to mine own protection.

GRATIANO. Well, do you so; let not me take him, then;
For if I do, I'll mar the young clerk's pen.

ANTONIO. I am the unhappy subject of these quarrels.

PORTIA. Sir, grieve not you; you are welcome notwithstanding.

BASSANIO. Portia, forgive me this enforced wrong;
And, in the hearing of these many friends,
I swear to thee, even by thine own fair eyes,
Wherein I see myself,—

PORTIA. Mark you but that!
In both my eyes he doubly sees himself;
In each eye, one:—swear by your double self,
And there's an oath of credit.

BASSANIO. Nay, but hear me:
Pardon this fault, and by my soul I swear
I never more will break an oath with thee.

ANTONIO. I once did lend my body for his wealth;[371]
Which, but for him that had your husband's ring,
Had quite miscarried: I dare be bound again,
My soul upon the forfeit, that your lord
Will never more break faith advisedly.[372]

---

[369] The "candles of the night" are the Moon and stars. So in *Romeo and Juliet*, iii. 5: "Night's candles are burnt out, and jocund day stand tiptoe on the misty mountain-tops."

[370] *Advised*, as before, for *cautious* or *circumspect*. See page 24, note 31.—*Well*, here, has the force of *very*.

[371] That is, for his *welfare* or his *good*. *Wealth* is only another form of *weal*: we say indifferently common-*weal* or common-*wealth*; and the commonwealth is the good that men have in common.—*Which*, in the next line, refers to the *loan* of Antonio's body.

[372] *Advisedly* is *deliberately*; much the same as in note 370.

PORTIA. Then you shall be his surety. Give him this
    And bid him keep it better than the other.
ANTONIO. Here, Lord Bassanio; swear to keep this ring.
BASSANIO. By Heaven, it is the same I gave the doctor!
PORTIA. I had it of him: pardon me, Bassanio;
    For, by this ring, the doctor lay with me.
NERISSA. And pardon me, my gentle Gratiano;
    For that same scrubbed boy, the doctor's clerk,
    In lieu of this,[373] last night did lie with me.
GRATIANO. Why, this is like the mending of highways
    In summer, where the ways are fair enough:
    What, are we cuckolds ere we have deserved it?
PORTIA. Speak not so grossly.—You are all amazed:
    Here is a letter; read it at your leisure;
    It comes from Padua, from Bellario:
    There you shall find that Portia was the doctor,
    Nerissa there her clerk: Lorenzo here
    Shall witness I set forth as soon as you
    And even but now return'd; I have not yet
    Enter'd my house.—Antonio, you are welcome;
    And I have better news in store for you
    Than you expect: unseal this letter soon;
    There you shall find three of your argosies
    Are richly come to harbour suddenly:[374]
    You shall not know by what strange accident
    I chanced on this letter.
ANTONIO. I am dumb.
BASSANIO. Were you the doctor and I knew you not?
GRATIANO. Were you the clerk that is to make me cuckold?
NERISSA. Ay, but the clerk that never means to do it,
    Unless he live until he be a man.
BASSANIO. Sweet doctor, you shall be my bed-fellow:
    When I am absent, then lie with my wife.
ANTONIO. Sweet lady, you have given me life and living;[375]
    For here I read for certain that my ships
    Are safely come to road.[376]

---

[373] *In lieu of,* again, in its old sense of *in return for,* or in *consideration of.* See page 90, note 334.

[374] *Suddenly* for *unexpectedly;* as in the *Litany* we pray to be delivered from "*sudden* death."

[375] Life and the *means of living.* Portia has given Antonio *life* in delivering him from the clutches of Shylock.

[376] In ii. 5, when Shylock is bid forth to Bassanio's supper, and Launcelot urges him to go, because "my young master doth expect your reproach," Shylock replies, "So do I his." Of course he expects that reproach through the bankruptcy of Antonio. This would seem to infer that Shylock has some hand in getting up the reports of Antonio's "losses at

PORTIA. How now, Lorenzo!
    My clerk hath some good comforts too for you.
NERISSA. Ay, and I'll give them him without a fee.—
    There do I give to you and Jessica,
    From the rich Jew, a special deed of gift,
    After his death, of all he dies possess'd of.
LORENZO. Fair ladies, you drop manna in the way
    Of starved people.
PORTIA. It is almost morning,
    And yet I am sure you are not satisfied
    Of these events at full. Let us go in;
    And charge us there upon inter'gatories,[377]
    And we will answer all things faithfully.
GRATIANO. Let it be so: the first inter'gatory
    That my Nerissa shall be sworn on is,
    Whether till the next night she had rather stay,
    Or go to bed now, being two hours to day:
    But were the day come, I should wish it dark,
    That I were couching with the doctor's clerk.
    Well, while I live I'll fear no other thing
    So sore as keeping safe Nerissa's ring. [*Exeunt.*]

THE END

---

sea"; which reports, at least some of them, turn out false in the end. Further than this, the Poet leaves us in the dark as to how those reports grew into being and gained belief. Did he mean to have it understood that the Jew exercised his cunning and malice in plotting and preparing them? It appears, at all events, that Shylock knew they were coming, before they came. Yet I suppose the natural impression from the play is, that he lent the ducats and took the bond, on a mere chance of coming at his wish. But he would hardly grasp so eagerly at a bare possibility of revenge, without using means to turn it into something more. This would mark him with much deeper lines of guilt. Why, then, did not Shakespeare bring the matter forward more prominently? Perhaps it was because the doing so would have made Shylock appear too deep a criminal for the degree of interest which his part was meant to carry in the play. In other words, the health of the drama as a work of *comic* art required his criminality to be kept in the background. He comes very near overshadowing the other characters too much, as it is. And Shylock's character is *essentially tragic*; there is none of the proper timber of comedy in him.

[377] In the Court of Queen's Bench, when a complaint is made against a person for a "contempt," the practice is that, before sentence is finally pronounced, he is sent into the Crown Office, and, being there "charged upon interrogatories," he is made to swear that he will "answer all things faithfully."—LORD CAMPBELL.